Paranormal
Missouri

Show Me Your Monsters

Jason Offutt

Schiffer Publishing Ltd®

4880 Lower Valley Road, Atglen, Pennsylvania 19310

Ouija is a registered trademark of Parker Brothers Games
"Does this man have a piece of an extraterrestrial craft?" originally appeared in the
September-October 2008 issue of Fate Magazine and is printed here by permission.

Schiffer Books are available at special discounts for bulk purchases for sales promotions or premiums. Special editions, including personalized covers, corporate imprints, and excerpts can be created in large quantities for special needs. For more information contact the publisher:

Published by Schiffer Publishing Ltd.
4880 Lower Valley Road
Atglen, PA 19310
Phone: (610) 593-1777; Fax: (610) 593-2002
E-mail: Info@schifferbooks.com

For the largest selection of fine reference books on this and related subjects, please visit our web site at
www.schifferbooks.com
We are always looking for people to write books on new and related subjects. If you have an idea for a book please contact us at the above address.

This book may be purchased from the publisher.
Include $5.00 for shipping.
Please try your bookstore first.
You may write for a free catalog.

In Europe, Schiffer books are distributed by
Bushwood Books
6 Marksbury Ave.
Kew Gardens
Surrey TW9 4JF England
Phone: 44 (0) 20 8392-8585; Fax: 44 (0) 20 8392-9876
E-mail: info@bushwoodbooks.co.uk
Website: www.bushwoodbooks.co.uk

Copyright © 2010 Jason Offutt
All photos unless otherwise noted are by the author
Library of Congress Control Number: 2010930657

Designed by Stephanie Daugherty
Type set in Informal Roman/New Baskerville BT/Humanst521 BT

ISBN: 978-0-7643-3577-8
Printed in The United States of America

Contents

Contents

Contents

Dedication

*T*his book is dedicated to my wife, Kimberly, who supports the fact that I hang out in cemeteries at 2 a.m., my children who are asleep at the time and have no idea what Daddy does at night, and my agent who … well, I don't have an agent and, even if I did, he or she probably wouldn't hang out with me in cemeteries, so thanks for nothing. But, mostly, this book is for all the people who've experienced something they can't explain and have taken the time to share it with me. Thank you.

Acknowledgments

*I*would like to thank Ryan Straub, Chris Black, Margie Kay, Belinda Clark-Ache, Kim Luney, Sean Maples, and Dale Brendel.

Foreword

*I*f you have not yet heard of the Missouri writer, Jason Offutt, then you are in for a great reading treat. He can tell an exciting story while reporting a tantalizing tale of the paranormal.

Whether you are ready for having a last fishing trip with Grandpa, checking into a secret UFO base at Jefferson City, Missouri, observing Night People, learning about Black-Eyed children, hearing about a UFO crash near Sikeston, Missouri, or encountering the screams of two alien sisters whose insect voices terrify, these writings will hold your interest from beginning to end. Jason Offutt has a knack for giving the reader an account that is exciting, entertaining, unusual, and educational all in one sitting. He is a good writer, and his prose sparkles with imaginative insights into the oftentimes-macabre material he investigates in the state of Missouri. There is always something strangely surreal happening in Missouri and this book is a good introduction to some of them.

Part of the charm of this book will be found in its unusual topics, and the other part will be found in the manner in which the topics are covered and shared with the reader. Whether you are interested in reading about the paranormal, UFOs, extraterrestrials, or other things that go bump in the night, you are more than likely to discover something to your personal liking in this well-written book. There are certainly weird things in Missouri, and Jason Offutt will share them with you. Just turn the page.

Lee Prosser

Writer of the "Bide One's Time" column at Ghostvillage.com and author of *Missouri Hauntings*, *Branson Hauntings*, *Missouri UFOs*, and the memoir, *Isherwood, Bowles, Vedanta, Wicca, and Me*

Introduction

D arkness surrounds us.
  We all see shadowy shapes lurking in our periphery, hear creaks on the floor of a night-filled house, and wonder if things lurk near us in the corners of our room ... and in the corners of our consciousness. That's normal. So are the explanations, if you're ready to accept as reality demons, ghosts, gray aliens and maybe even a fairy or two.

My question: Do you *believe*?

Over the past year, I've driven thousands of miles across Missouri, spoken with hundreds of eyewitnesses of paranormal events, walked through dozens of cemeteries, Victorian mansions, and Civil War battlefields, and have interviewed people from across the state. Each of these spots and each of these people have something in common – they've all experienced something science can't explain.

Why Missouri? I live here.

Throughout my investigations of haunted places, homeowners, tour guides, psychics, and tourists have asked me the same question: Do I believe in ghosts? The word "believe" bothers me. You only believe in something because you don't have proof it exists. If you can see it, you don't have to believe in it ... it's just there. I've seen a ghost – yep, a full-bodied apparition – so I don't have to believe in ghosts, I know they're real. But everything else? I'm just looking for proof.

Unfortunately, so far, there's really no scientific test for ghosts, demons, or angels – which is too bad. I've interviewed enough credible eyewitnesses about haunted houses, possessions, and poltergeist activity to convince me something's going on outside our normal realm of perception.

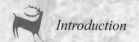

Personally, I've walked through haunted buildings and stepped into spots that were at least twenty degrees lower than the surrounding air. Oh, and each time the building wasn't air-conditioned ... and it was July. I've smelled cigar smoke in places where cigar smoke couldn't have existted (a museum, a historic Civil War jail, and a 150-year-old bed and breakfast when no one else was in the building). I've heard a friend's name called from the blank, concrete corner of an unfinished basement.

Have I ever been afraid? Not really. Just uncomfortable. Well, except maybe the phantom skateboarder who closed upon me so fast I jumped off a walking trail at 6 a.m. There was no one behind me. That at least made me nervous. My wife laughed because, unlike me, she hadn't heard the skateboard wheels grinding on the concrete path behind us.

But because of this, I'm ready for anything. I don't believe in the paranormal – I'm convinced it exists.

There are 43 stories in this book, some of them long and some of them short; some about ghosts, some about Bigfoot, some about UFOs, and some about stuff even I think is weird – but they all have one thing in common, they're real. I didn't include many of the well-known haunted spots in Missouri, like the Lemp Mansion in St. Louis, Union Cemetery in Kansas City, and Wilson's Creek Battlefield near Springfield, because they're famous. People already know about them. Most of the stories in *Paranormal Missouri* are obscure. I included them because you *don't* know about them. Like the possibility of a UFO base in our state capital, the Night People of Orrick, and Bigfoot encounters near Pleasant Hill and in Southeast Missouri. During my research I visited a number of these spots, like Gravity Hill near Freeman, just to see if the paranormal claims are true. I also looked into the history of the events, and interviewed the people they occurred to. And you know what? I'm a little creeped out.

But before you step any further into the world of the unknown, you need to understand what you are, or are not, dealing with. First, the terms paranormal and supernatural mean basically the same thing, something that's beyond the day-to-day perception of the average human being. Okay, so the Dalai Lama, the Pope, and *Ghostbuster*'s Dr. Peter Venkman aren't necessarily average human beings – or, in the case of Dr. Peter Venkman, real – but even the Dalai Lama and the Pope know more about the paranormal world than we do. Trust me, religion is where the paranormal starts.

So how do you judge what is, and what is not, paranormal? By weeding out the obvious: the wind, crickets, someone's weight on old floorboards, a nearby airport making the EMF meter go crazy, mist/dust/insects causing orbs in photographs, your mind playing tricks on you, someone just seeking attention, that meatball, mozzarella, pepperoni and jalapeno sub you ate before the investigation – stuff like that. If you can look at these points, as well as pesky things like common sense and physics, and aren't able to explain a strange occurrence, then you've got something. My dad always told me the weird noises I heard in the night were just the house settling. He was probably right. Well, except for all the Shadow People in my room.

Before we dive into the world of the paranormal, a world you'll soon find has unnervingly wrapped itself around the lives of many Missourians, let's know what we're getting ourselves into. Although no one knows the true answers to what any of the following topics I cover in *Paranormal Missouri* are (and if they claim to, don't give them any money), here are some explanations as to what they might be:

Ghosts

For uncounted centuries, unconnected cultures across the globe consider ghosts to be spirits of the dead. Can they all be wrong? Christianity says spirits in Heaven and Hell can't communicate with the living; angels and demons can. Maybe what you think is the ghost of Grandma Mae staring at you from the foot of your bed is something a bit more sinister.

Electronic Voice Phenomena

Thomas Edison thought his phonograph might be a way to communicate with the dead. Recording devices have long been used to trap unheard voices – the voices of the dead – electronically. I've heard them. Go ahead, place an audio recorder in your bedroom at night and see what it has to say to you the next morning.

UFOs

Are just what the name states – Unidentified Flying Objects. Anything you see in the sky and can't identify is a UFO. It might be an airplane, meteorite, balloon, strange cloud formation, or the planet Venus. Of course, it could also be an extraterrestrial craft. We don't know. It's unidentified.

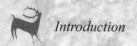

Ouija Boards

The talking board, now sold by the toy company Hasbro/Parker Brothers, is anything but a toy. This method of divination has been around since at least 1100 B.C. It has been used to speak to the dead ... and some things that have never lived, nor died. Use with caution. No, scratch that. Don't use one at all.

Cryptozoology

Animals unknown to science or are believed extinct. Bigfoot, lake monsters, the Mongolian Death Worm, el chupacabra, living dinosaurs, the thylacine are all creatures that are hidden – like Bigfoot – or are presumed extinct – like the thylacine. Of course, Western science thought the mountain gorilla and the giant panda were myths. They were wrong.

Strange Humanoids

Fairies, gnomes, earth spirits, and Black-Eyed Kids are human-like entities that have stalked our earthy plane for centuries lurking just outside our normal view of what we think is reality.

Extraterrestrials

Any living cell, plant, animal, or bug-eyed monster that comes from outside our atmosphere.

Welcome to *Paranormal Missouri: Show Me Your Monsters*. The following stories are true. Follow me as I investigate ghosts, talk to people on the other side, and search for the unknown. Oh, and if at any time during our time together you feel uncomfortable, eat some garlic. It couldn't hurt.

1

Electronic Voice Phenomena

Sitting at a table in the vast dining hall at Springfield's Pythian Castle, psychic Dawn Newlan of the Ozark Paranormal Society played voices the group recorded there in 2005. Some of the voices were clear, some muffled, but all of them had something in common – they were recorded when no one was home.

Electronic Voice Phenomenon, or EVP, is an unexpected sound that appears on an audio recording. EVPs have been around since the 1920s when Thomas Edison tried to develop a machine to talk with the dead. Today, ghost hunters place tape and digital audio recorders in empty rooms to capture the voices of earthbound spirits.

And Pythian Castle is rife with spirits. The castle, a three-story stone structure built in 1913, has been an orphanage, hospital, WWII Army headquarters where German POWs were interrogated, and a bed and breakfast. "In the basement, we've heard two or three different voices," Dawn said. "We've actually got voices on tape."

From Dawn's recordings come the moans, "I am not myself," "punish him," and "I'll kill him." Dawn also played whispers, laughter, and the faint sound of a man hissing, "It's Okay." All were gathered in empty rooms. "Each one of the ghost hunting people have gotten something unusual here," said Tamara Finocchiaro, co-owner of the castle.

Ghost hunter Ryan Straub also records EVPs. Ryan has picked up EVPs in desolate Hazel Ridge Cemetery near Brunswick. "I sat it just like that," he said, placing a recorder atop a weatherworn tombstone. "And we walked away from it. The next morning we listened to it and it sounded like chipmunks. I slowed it down and it was a little girl singing 'Ring Around the Rosie.'" The tombstone was next to the graves of children.

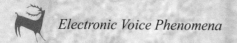

Springfield's Pythian Castle, a three-story stone structure built in 1913, has been an orphanage, hospital, WWII Army headquarters, and a bed and breakfast. It's also rife with spirits – some of whom like to talk.

Ryan Straub (pictured) and his paranormal research group, Tir Firnath, collect EVPs in Hazel Ridge Cemetery where they've captured the voices of little girls singing. *Photo courtesy of Ryan Straub*

Carol Mullins works for the University of Central Missouri's housing department, mainly in Laura J. Yeater Hall. She'd worked there about five years when she played for me her EVPs. Legend has it the building is haunted. The ground floor of Yeater is empty, and its banquet room generally remains quiet. That's where Carol likes to collect EVPs. "I put my tape recorder in there and there was a moan," she said. "It wasn't the wind… It was a moan. It was a moan of pain. A lot of people say that's

Does the ghost of Laura J. Yeater haunt the residence hall at the University of Central Missouri that bears her name? Something does.

the radiator, but the radiators aren't on here over the summer." Carol has also collected EVPs in her Yeater Hall office at night. "There were like a dozen girls giggling outside my door," she said. "It was the summer. How were there girls giggling outside my door?"

What are the voices picked up by these ghost hunters? The sounds of restless spirits? Demons? Past events seeping into the present? Or is someone just playing? "All the tape recordings, it's just weird," Carol said. "I can't explain it."

Want to capture an EVP? Place a tape recorder in your living room, hit "record" and leave the house. But later, as you're about to press "play," just remember, you might not like what you hear.

2

1941 UFO Crash
Near Sikeston

A mysterious aircraft crashes in a rural area. The FBI recovers strange bodies. The wreck is whisked off by the military. Documents are missing. This isn't the story of Roswell, New Mexico.

Linda was born in Sikeston, Missouri, a town known for Lambert's Café, the home of "throwed rolls," and the Southeast Missouri Agricultural Museum. It's not known for a UFO crash. Information Linda has uncovered may change that. When Linda was young, her father worked at the Missouri Institute of Aeronautics in Sikeston and may have been privy to information of a downed UFO between Cape Girardeau and Sikeston six years before the alleged crash of a flying saucer at Roswell. "I would like to think if your father knew something, he'd share it," she said. "But I have no answers."

In the spring of 1941, at about 9 p.m., Baptist minister William Huffman of Cape Girardeau was asked to deliver last rights to the pilot and passengers of an aircraft that crashed about 15 miles outside of town, in the direction of Sikeston, according to a letter from Huffman's granddaughter Charlette Mann to UFO investigator Leo Stringfield.

When Rev. Huffman arrived, police, fire officials, the military, and the FBI poured over the crash site of a disc-shaped craft. The pilot and passengers were "little gray people" with large, almond-shaped black eyes, according to Mann's letter. Huffman was sworn to secrecy. So, it seems, was everyone else.

Linda discovered the area's fire, sheriff, and police departments have no records for 1941. No records exist for the Missouri

Institute of Aeronautics. And stories have been removed from microfilm issues of the *Sikeston Herald* around the time of the alleged crash.

"I thought that was unusual," Linda said. "I had gone to other dates and they did not have problems. And looking for an original for that paper, it's not anywhere." So Linda did what any good researcher does. She started asking questions. "One source spoke about 'little people' that died and were transported from the alleged crash site," she said. "An unrelated source spoke about a fairly recent visit by a former associate of the Missouri Institute of Aeronautics. In her words, 'There is a man – somewhat confused – who said he 'picked up the bodies' of crash victims from the base."

Linda found that man in a locked wing of a Sikeston nursing home. "I identified myself and my father's name," she said. "The man's face went from a blank look to an ear-to-ear grin. 'Your Dad was my crew chief – that was so long ago.'" After a few questions, Linda was satisfied this man had known her father. "I told the aging patient I would like to discuss the Missouri Institute of Aeronautics and the air crashes that were never reported," she said. "The blank look returned to his face. 'I do not know, I do not know.' He was lost again and we did not reconnect." After the man died, she discovered this is the man who had spoken with the "unrelated source" about the bodies.

These are the interviews that keep Linda's research going. "I get bits and pieces of stories," she said. "Evidence to either prove or disprove the event only leads to more questions. Two senior Sikestonians recall talk of the crash of an unidentified craft, others recall a meteor crash, and still others recall no incident. I continue the search." But not forever. "I don't think it's within my ability uncover the truth," Linda said. "I know this is not something one person can solve."

You can contact Linda through her website, www.seeking-moinfo.com.

3

The Ghosts of Workman Chapel

A deep sea of gray clouds masked the setting sun as we pulled into the chapel's dirt drive. There were six of us on the ghost hunt. Myself, audio/visual engineer Will Murphy, and four Northwest Missouri State University freshmen. Freshmen? Hey, they were doing it for a grade.

We parked under the limbs of two trees that had grown old next to the chapel. In one, according to legend, a woman was hanged

From Civil War soldiers patrolling nearby corn fields to Shadow People, strange things happen at Workman Chapel and Cemetery about eleven miles outside Maryville.

and anyone sitting in a car beneath that spot will hear her shoes scraping on the roof. *Urban* legend, yeah. But the freshmen were still nervous.

Workman Chapel, just north of Maryville, was quiet in the dusk, its black, glassless windows and open door frame slightly beyond uninviting. We were there to find the ghosts of the woman and two Civil War soldiers who reportedly ride their horses in the chapel's cemetery.

Former Northwest student Jessica Lavicky heard the horses. Her dog heard something, too. "We walked down to the cemetery and the dog started running back and forth like it was playing with somebody," Jessica said. "But it wasn't playing with us."

John Workman built the chapel in 1901. He's buried there. Workman's descendent, Lester Workman, is caretaker of the chapel. "It's been empty for years," he said. "It's been 50 years or better." But people have heard church bells peal at the chapel and have seen black, human shapes dancing on the tombstones. That's what we were there to see.

Murphy, engineer of Northwest's Mass Communication department, brought digital cameras, a digital video camera, digital audio recorder and a voltmeter. The cameras were to capture "orbs." These balls of light you can't see with the naked eye sometimes appear in digital pictures. Some people claim orbs are pictures of ghosts. Others say they're light reflecting off dust, insects, or moisture.

The video and audio equipment were to record disembodied voices. Freshmen Kayla Lindsey, Katie Pierce, and Harrison Sissel* shot still pictures in the now black cemetery while Mallory Riley wandered with the voltmeter, trying to pick up energy fluctuations some associate with ghosts.

Then the fun began.

Katie and Kayla called me over. Katie had just taken two pictures. One had orbs. The other didn't. Dust and insects should have been in both. Had she captured the image of a ghost?

Who knows?

"Oh my God," Kayla said as Mallory walked past with the voltmeter. Will said the meter can generally pick up .14 volts out of the air; more around an electrical source. If the meter went past .40, Mallory was supposed to say something. "It's gone up to eighty," Kayla said. Ninety. One hundred. One hundred fifteen. The meter went to 120 before Will pointed out they'd been walking toward utility lines. Easy mistake.

Then Harrison ran into one of the great problems of ghost hunting in a crowd mixed with boys, girls, and, maybe, monsters. He had to go to the bathroom and he didn't want to go alone. Kayla laughed.

"He can't pee in front of ghosts."

Maybe it was time to go. We drove back to the university. Did we find evidence of ghosts? The orbs were interesting, but inconclusive and debatable. We didn't record voices. And we didn't detect anomalous energy fields. But, it was fun. Would any of us go again?

"There's an abandoned insane asylum near Iowa," Will said after the freshmen had gone. "People say they hear human screams coming from it at night. Want to go?"

Heck yes.

* Harrison, now graduated, has yet to live this down.

4

The Curious Story of Jap Herron

"That the story of Jap Herron and the two short stories which pre-
ceded it are the actual post-mortem work of Samuel L. Clemens, known
to the world as Mark Twain, we do not for one moment doubt."

– Emily Grant Hutchings
"The Coming of Jap Herron" (1917)

Mark Twain, died in 1910. During the mid-to late-1800s, Twain's novels, essays, and short stories made him a world-wide celebrity. Through financial failures and personal tragedy, Twain, who in 1875 pecked out the first novel ever written on a typewriter, *The Adventures of Tom Sawyer*, never stopped writing. Maybe even after death.

Emily Grant Hutchings, a struggling novelist, teacher, and writer for St. Louis newspapers, claimed Twain dictated his last novel and two short stories – "Daughter of Mars" and "Up the Furrow to For-tune" – to her one letter at a time between 1915 and 1917 through a Ouija board.

"They got on the Ouija board and supposedly had this conversa-tion," said Henry Sweets, curator of the Twain Museum in Hannibal. Many conversations. Twain supposedly dictated chapter after chapter – including revisions – to Hutchings and spiritualist medium Lola V. Hays, according to Hutchings' Foreword. Why would Twain pick Hutchings to pen his new works? She was from Twain's boyhood home of Hannibal.

The book, *Jap Herron*, was published by Mitchell Kennerley in 1917 as "a novel written from the Ouija board – Mark Twain via Emily Grant Hutchings." Harper & Brothers, owners of the copyright on the pen name "Mark Twain," sued Kennerley in 1918.

Struggling novelist Emily Grant Hutchings claims to have written the book, The Coming of Jap Herron, between 1915 and 1917 with the ghost of Mark Twain through a Ouija board.

JAP HERRON

A NOVEL WRITTEN FROM THE OUIJA BOARD

[MARK TWAIN via EMILY GRANT HUTCHINGS]

WITH AN INTRODUCTION

THE COMING OF JAP HERRON

NEW YORK
MCMXVII

Given the nature of Ouija boards – although not officially classified as a game by the Supreme Court until 1920 – Harper & Brothers had a strong case. But, according to a story in the July 28, 1918 *New York Times*, the case was about more than an issue of copyright. "We will put the issue up to the Supreme Court," said James N. Rosenberg, an attorney for Harper & Brothers. "We will have a final ruling on immortality."

Part of Harper & Brothers' case revolved around the fact that Twain had written in the books, "What is Man?" and "The Mysterious Stranger," that he didn't acknowledge life after death. "He refused to believe in a spirit world," the *New York Times* printed. "He refused to be a spook. Judge or jury must weigh that fact."

But the case never went to trial and life after death remains in the realm of religion. Kennerley and Hutchings agreed to stop distribution of *Jap Herron* and destroy all known copies and Harper & Brothers dropped the lawsuit.

So the question remains, was the novel written by Mark Twain? In *Contact with the Other World*, by James H. Hyslop (1919), Hyslop details many sessions with Hays and Hutchings at a Ouija board and saw evidence Mark Twain had dictated a novel from the Great Beyond. But, really, who knows?

Despite the Supreme Court ruling, in some circles the Ouija board isn't a toy. It's a gateway to the spirit world. So beware, you may conjure something a little more dangerous than a humorist from Hannibal. "There is no instruction booklet for the Ouija," according to Sharon Scott and Mary Carothers in 'Toys, Games, and Hobbies in North America.' "There is only one rule that everyone knows: Never play alone."

As a sidenote, not all copies of Jap Herron were destroyed. One is in the Mark Twain Museum in Hannibal.

You can also find Jap Herron online at www.spiritwritings.com/JapHerronTwain. pdf#search='jap%20herron'.

5

The Little Ghost of Charleston

The following real-life ghost story is a reader's experience. It happened to Samuel J. Saladino, now of South Beloit, Illinois, when he lived in Charleston, Missouri, in the early 1990s. This is his story:

I was working the late shift, and at about 8 p.m. my now ex-wife woke me to ask if we could go to a restaurant. We were living with my sister and her husband and I asked my sister if she'd like to join us.

When we returned to the house, I sensed something wasn't right. We had Pomeranians we kept in the kitchen. Poms are yippie dogs, but tonight they were silent. I put my finger to my lips and my wife and sister looked at me. I put my finger to my ear and mouthed, "What do you hear?" They shrugged their shoulders and mouthed, "nothing." Then they realized the dogs weren't making any sound.

I motioned for them to stay where they were while I edged to the kitchen. The male Pom was sitting on the kitchen floor looking at something. I edged closer and saw a girl of about eleven, bent over looking at the dogs.

She had pigtails hanging over each shoulder, dangling above the heads of the dogs. They seemed to be watching the girl and would from time to time wag their tails. She wore a white blouse, a dark blue jumper, stockings and black strap shoes. To me, it must be a girl who lived in the neighborhood, had heard the dogs and let herself in.

I stepped into the doorway and said, "Hi." She looked up, our eyes met, and I have never seen such a look of terror in anyone's face before.

24

Then the dogs started barking.

She turned to run, and I said, "Wait." When she reached the door to the back yard she didn't stop and she ran through the solid door. I could see her running across the back yard, as if in full daylight, but this was 10 p.m. As she reached the end of the yard in front of some woods, the light started to swirl around her and everything disappeared into a dot and the darkness reclaimed the night.

I ran out to see if I could find where she had disappeared. There were two other dogs barking at the spot where she vanished. I can only assume they saw her, too.

My wife and sister caught up to me, screaming, "What's wrong?" I turned and their faces went white and they said, "You look like you've seen a ghost." How right they were.

There were no woods at the spot the little girl disappeared. The land had been cleared years before and was now a field. "You saw her didn't you?" my sister asked. "The little girl, dressed in a dark jumper, pigtails, about ten years old?"

She'd seen this girl since she'd moved into the house. She'd often see her peeking around the corner. At first she thought it was a neighbor girl, but she'd search and never find anyone.

Neighbors remembered an elderly lady who lived in the house years before my sister. They always saw her wearing her hair in pigtails, braided, one hanging over each shoulder. I often wonder if that elderly lady had passed on and simply returned to the place she loved most.

6

Tales from the Ouija Board

*T*he group of friends huddled around a game board, their fingers hovering over a small flittering planchet. It was the 1960s. Roland Sneed and his then-wife were in Kansas City from Oklahoma visiting her parents when someone decided it would be fun to play with the unknown. "My former wife and I spent several hours with friends using the Ouija board," Roland, now of Blue Springs, said. "Sometimes the planchet went very slow and sometimes it would go so fast that it would fly off the board. Some answers were cryptic, some muddled, and some very, very interesting."

Later, the couple slept in a seldom-used room in the old house. But the board wasn't finished playing. "My wife began making strange movements and then started talking in a voice not her own," Roland said. "I wasn't scared, but fascinated. I started asking questions about who she was and she replied that she was an ancestor of my wife. It is hard to know whether or not this was true. Specific facts were not given.

"After a while, my wife came out of this trance with beaded sweat on her brow and scared out of her mind. She said that she could feel the spirit trying to take over her body and had struggled against it until she got back into control. She refused to even look at a Ouija board after that."

Roland and his wife met what Dawn Newlan, a medium with the Ozark Paranormal Society, calls lower-level energies. "Generally, the things that come through always tell you they are a friend, a family member, a whatever," Newlan said, adding you should keep your distance. "Ouijas to me, and to most anyone who's been around one will tell you they are very dangerous," she said. "When someone plays with a board they begin to open up the doorways of communication with the other side."

Negative energies come through these doorways, Newlan said. Sometimes these energies are people who were bad in life, and sometimes they are demons. "Satan has his legions," Newlan said. "If you do not know how to discern good entities from bad entities, that's when you wind up with your problems. What most people don't understand is that if you ask them a question, 'Hey what is my dog's name?' (The name) is in your head," she said. "That spirit can take it out of your head and give you what you want to hear."

Newlan speaks from experience. She's used a Ouija. "I was young and stupid," she said. "Something came through and told me it was my grandma. It told me it loved me and wanted to visit me." Later the board began spelling 'evil, evil, evil, evil.' "A Ouija board, until you experience it, is a fascination," Newlan said. "Your common sense tells you, you really shouldn't be doing it, but your curiosity pushes you. Once it scares the hell out of you, you'll quit."

But some people believe the Ouija board works, not through spirits, but through the subconscious mind of the user. "It's my preferred explanation for the phenomenon," Marleigh, who posted on from-the-shadows.blogspot.com, said. "One or all of the participants is moving the pointer, subconsciously. I've had it happen to me where you will ask, "What is your name?" and I will think a specific name, say, "Jason," and without me pushing the pointer, the name Jason will be spelled out. This could explain Ouija board happenings."

Maybe. I don't want to find out.

7

Does This Man Have a Piece of an Extraterrestrial Craft?

Bob White found something strange in 1985. He can explain it – and often does – but people don't take him seriously. *That* is something he can't explain. The object he found was metallic, about 7 1/2 inches long and resembles petrified wood. What makes it special to White is that he saw it ejected from a strange light … a light he's certain was a UFO.

"This thing came down out of the sky," White, of Reeds Spring, Missouri, said. "It was glowing like it was on fire. There's no doubt in my mind it wasn't anything of this earth. It couldn't be."

White took the object to government lab after government lab – including Los Alamos National Laboratory – and after two decades of being brushed off, someone is taking him seriously.

Mark W. Allin of The Above Network (www.AboveTopSecret. com, an Internet discussion board that boasts 127,794 members who discuss alternative news topics) has recently come to White's aid … partly because he knows an object like this has been seen before.

"When you take into account the eyewitness testimony of Bob, who has passed three polygraph tests, this object becomes very unique," Allin said. "When you add the discovery of a formerly classified military report that describes an extremely similar event that also produced an object that is extremely similar to the Bob White object, it just gets bizarre."

Then there's White's conviction that the object was made by an intelligence not of this earth.

"Everything points in the direction of extraterrestrials," White said. "Most of the analysis says that this thing is nothing organic from anything in or outside of earth's atmosphere. There's no explanation whatsoever."

Bob White of Reeds Spring claims to have seen this object fall from a UFO in 1985.

And that's where, until Allin stepped in, White's evidence ended. Although a few scientists have agreed to look at the object, White can't find one who'll say what it is … at least on the record.

"It's been analyzed by eight major labs, including Los Alamos (National Laboratories in 1996)," White said. "I was told by one of the older scientists it was extraterrestrial, definitely. Then he later denied he said it. His bosses told him not to even talk about it."

That's one of the points that intrigued Allin – the mystery. Why have all the labs, all the scientists, given different answers?

"I remembered reading about this thing years ago and wanted to see if anything conclusive had been determined about it. Turns out that Larry Cekander, Bob's close friend, joined the discussion (on www.AboveTopSecret.com) and told us about all the conflicting reports and test results they had received," Allin said. "After reading about all of that I decided it might be a good idea to apply the resources of The Above Network toward getting a definitive answer as to what this thing is, where it came from and how old it is."

According to a report from Colm Kelleher of the National Institute for Discovery Science, tests conducted at New Mexico Tech in 1996, showed the object was close in composition to a commercial aluminum-casting alloy. "There are no anomalies in the results of this analysis," the report stated. The test results were good enough for nuclear physicist Stanton Friedman, author of the UFO books *Crash at Corona* and *Top Secret/Majic*.

"I was very favorably impressed with the testing procedures and results and can't argue with their conclusion that it was a more or less standard aluminum alloy with silicon and other materials," Friedman said. "The composition, hardness, density, etc. all seemed to check out. I have no reason to doubt Bob's story, but see no reason to say that the material is clearly of E.T. origin."

But White has always contested the New Mexico Tech tests, and The Above Network has enlisted an independent Ph.D. metallurgist who has agreed to analyze White's object. Allin said he's not interested in bringing more attention to the object; he just wants to find out what it is and where it's from.

"There is a lot of speculation that the results of some of the previous tests were not presented accurately," Allin said. "By hiring an independent scientist who answers to no one but himself we will be certain the results of his work will be genuine and accurate."

But after reviewing the results of previous tests, Allin's independent Ph.D. metallurgist decided in January that more analysis wasn't necessary.

"The recommendation is not to pursue any additional testing since the object possesses low quality metallurgic properties, exhibits low quality processing, and test results show that it originated from the earth," Allin wrote in an e-mail.

White is not satisfied with the metallurgist's recommendation.

"ATS did not do any tests as they said they were going to," White said. "All they did was a review of others."

The Bob White object is metallic, seven and a half inches long, and resembles petrified wood.

White has asked his debunkers – if this is a manufactured object of earth origin – to make one themselves. So far, he has no takers.

"As of yet, no reply from anyone," he said. "So since I am the only man who can make one I guess this makes me the smartest man in the world huh?"

Former president of the Institute for UFO Research, Franklin Carter, now a member of the Disclosure Project and the Mutual UFO Network, is familiar with White and is puzzled by the problems he's faced.

"I know he's had a difficult time in trying to get someone to help him in the UFO community," Carter said. "You'd think with all the clamor for hard evidence, people would be crawling all over themselves to get to it."

Carter was involved with a UFO contactee conference hosted by the University of Wyoming when he met White.

"I believe his story," Carter said. "I have no question he found this thing and it fell off something in the sky."

Carter, who works in the animal pharmaceutical industry, also tried to get someone in the science field to look at White's object.

"I had some excellent contacts," he said. "I talked to some of them about it. 'Well, we don't want to get involved in UFOs, but we'll get you the data' … I'm still waiting."

White said the object heats and cools rapidly and picks up radio signals – AM and FM. And, during a UFO convention in Nevada, it disabled the electronics in a casino's hotel safe – three times.

"They ordered us not to walk through the casino with it," White said.

White briefly opened the Museum of the Unexplained in Reeds Spring, the object being the centerpiece, but didn't make enough money to keep the museum open. Things changed for White in 2000 when he received information about a government report from the 1940s made available in 1998 through the Freedom of Information Act entitled, "Flying Saucer from Denmark." The report describes an object almost identical to White's object in appearance and composition recovered in the 1940s.

But it wasn't just the laboratory denial that got Allin and Carter interested in White's case, it was his whole story.

While driving through Colorado at 2 a.m., White and a friend saw a light on the roadside near the Colorado/Utah border. The light, White said, shouldn't have been there.

"It was a huge light on the ground," White said. "The light I saw was the size of a three-story building." White, sitting in the passenger seat, watched his friend slow the car. "She was scared."

White's friend turned off the car's engine and headlights. "We coasted as close to this item as we could," he said. "She didn't want to stop but we did."

They sat in the car, looking at the bright light when White's friend turned on the headlights.

"Then the thing shot up in the sky," White said, and merged with other lights hovering in the sky. "It was two tubular neon lights with a blue light in between. The other light shot across the sky and disappeared in seconds. I know we don't have anything that moves that fast or that silently."

As the lights streaked across the sky, another light – small and orange – broke free and fell to earth.

"This thing was ejected from it," White said. "If this thing had just fallen it would have shot miles from me. It came down at an angle and kind of skimmed the hillside. When I came across it, it was still glowing."

Bob White's book, *UFO Hard Evidence*, and DVD, "The Bob White Experience," are available at his Web site, www.ufohardevidence.com, along with a petition for a "Congressional Hearing on the Bob White Evidence."

8

Is Your House Haunted?

Better Tell Your Real-Estate Agent

Khristina Lorenz bought her first home in September. It's small, "but, hey, it's mine." The two-bedroom house sits beside a large, old cemetery in a calm Independence neighborhood; traffic on the busy Noland Road humming nearby. Her house is busy, too – but not with traffic.

Khristina bought the house from her boyfriend. He'd told stories that, late at night, doors would rattle like someone was trying to open them. But no one was ever there.

"I didn't really believe it," Khristina said. Then she heard the doors shake one night. "He's right. It was really loud like someone was about to break down the door or something."

Then the ghostly intrusions started happening when Khristina was home with her children, her boyfriend, or when she was alone. "My radio will just turn on by itself and my CD will start playing," she said. "A few times when I have come home after my part-time job in the evening, the radio has been on and the sound isn't going but the equalizer lights are going crazy."

Khristina may have bought a haunted house. In some states, there are laws against that. Depending on a state's definition of "stigmatized property," the seller has to tell the buyer whether or not their house is infested with termites, or poltergeists. Stigmatized property simply means something happened on the property that could psychologically affect the buyer. That includes a natural death, murder, suicide, a previous owner had HIV/AIDS, a felony was committed on the property, and, in some states, ghosts.

Jeanne Goolsby, owner of Grand Avenue Bed and Breakfast, and her husband Michael bought a Victorian home in Carthage, Missouri. The home had a second floor, a basement, a beautiful smoking room, and a resident spirit – Albert. But they knew about Albert before they bought the house. "The lady before us kept trying to tell us about the ghost and I told her I did not want to know," Goolsby said. "(Michael) said he can't remember it being on any paperwork, but he knew about it from the owner. She told us."

In California, the seller has to disclose a stigma up to three years from the time it occurred. Texas has no law about it at all. But the 1991 New York appellate court tackled the supernatural in a decision (Stambovsky v. Ackley) that allowed a buyer to cancel a contract when he discovered there was a "poltergeist" in the house.

If you're buying a house in Missouri, there's a law about stigmatized property; a law that doesn't favor the buyer. It specifically states the seller isn't required to disclose a stigma – which probably includes the walls bleeding.

The walls of Khristina's house don't bleed, but her haunting has gotten more and more personal. "I have heard voices several times," she said. Her boyfriend never heard voices while he owned the home. "It sounds like a women's voice and a small child's voice. I can never really make out clearly what they are saying but have heard this often. The first few times I thought it was my son, but when I checked on him he was asleep, I heard the voices and he was still snoring."

So sleep tight, and let the buyer beware.

9

Margie Kay
Psychic Ghost Hunter

The room was dark and Margie Kay of Independence was afraid. Eleven-year-old Kay was in bed when something appeared in the room she shared with her sister; something that – at the time – she couldn't explain.

It was a human head.

"My deceased grandfather, who I've never met, appeared in my bedroom to me and my sister," she said. "Just his head. Glowing and floating at the end of my bed." The sisters were motionless, watching the bodiless head stare at them, but just for a moment. "We screamed bloody murder," Kay said. "My father came in and we tried to describe (the head) to him and he took us downstairs and showed us a picture in an album and it was him."

Her father was calm about the incident, but Kay didn't find out why until she was in her 20s. Her father was psychic. "I guess he was just waiting for me to bring the subject up," she said. "But I just remember it was scary at the time and I wasn't ready to deal with it."

Today, Kay is an author, radio talk show host, and paranormal investigator. She describes herself as "extremely psychic."

Independence psychic Margie Kay.
Photo courtesy of Margie Kay

"I'm clairaudient, clairvoyant, and clairsentient," Kay said, meaning she can hear things most people can't hear, see things most people can't see, and sense things most people can't sense.

But at eleven, she wasn't ready to see a floating head at the end of her bed – even though that wasn't her first paranormal experience. "As a very young child, I was afraid of a flower in the wallpaper in the corner of the room that resembled an Indian chief," she said. "I had no exposure to American Indians ... to that point. I called it Ha-Ha. Those were my first words." She heard drums and saw lights no one else could. "I was just terrified," she said. "My father figured I was either an American Indian or had something bad happen that involved Indians in a previous life."

As an adult, Kay went under past life regression to find out. "I remembered being a healer, a shaman, a woman and growing to a very old age with long gray hair," she said.

In 1987, she felt an intense pain, like something was trying to pop through her skin. "I had an umbilical hernia," Kay said. "I went to the surgeon and had to undergo emergency surgery." Some time after the surgery, she woke up alone in a hospital room. Soon, an intern came in to check her bandages. "When she pulled the bandages off, blood started squirting out of my stomach," Kay said.

The intern rushed to get a doctor, but Kay wasn't alone for long. "A very tall, older gentleman comes in the door and says, 'I'm from Unity Church, and is there anything I can help you with?'" The man, who said his name was John Paul, held Kay's hand, said a prayer and left the room. "Right after that, the doctor and nurse came in and the doctor pulled back the (bandages) and (the wound) is completely shut," Kay said. "Right then, I knew something was up."

Someone else must have known, too. Kay was kept in the hospital for three more days. "Not once did I see a nurse. Just once did I see that doctor," Kay said. "It was strange." The day Kay arrived home from the hospital, two people stopped by for an unannounced visit. She hadn't seen them in five years. "One said she worked for Unity Church," Kay said. "She said John Paul did work for Unity, but he's been dead for three years."

Kay's no stranger to the strange.

"As a child, I noticed that I was seeing things and hearing things that other people weren't," said Kay. "I saw auras around people and trees as a youngster."

And she saw UFOs. "I had sightings as a child," she said. "And as a child, I also felt I didn't belong here on this earth. I didn't know why I felt that way." In 1989, after reading books on UFOs, she suspected her 1987 umbilical hernia may have been an implanted alien device.

"I went to a person who specializes in regressing UFO abductees," she said. While undergoing regressive hypnotherapy, she said, she saw the event that would affect her life for decades. "I found myself in my 9-year-old body in a house we used to live in with lights coming in the window and then landing on the floor turning into small children," she said. "They floated me off the bed and through the window onto the grass. And we were all standing in the circle holding hands."

But she soon found the beings were not children. "They were aliens," she said. "What I thought was the moon above us was a gigantic ship. This white beam came down and took us up to this ship." The young Kay saw the earth grow smaller as the alien ship left the atmosphere. Then she said the ship left the solar system and landed on a barren planet dotted with brown grass and brown bushes. "I was sent with someone else that came off the ship," she said. "They sent us down the pathway to go to this school and handed us some books. I knew at that point that this was my school, and it was at this point the implant was put in. I also knew these beings came for me many, many times for training. "It happens to many people."

The aliens made it clear to Kay why they abduct humans. "They have told me several things," Kay said. "Their purpose is to raise the consciousness of humans and to also try to help protect us from ourselves – war and destroying the planet." Kay is a grandmother, and she said the aliens have also contacted her children and grandchildren.

Although Kay said the alien contact has given her physical problems, such as fibromyalgia, they have helped her, too, by increasing her psychic ability.

Because of her psychic ability, police agencies have called on Kay to help find missing persons. "I've worked 25 missing persons cases with big agencies and all were successful except one," she said. "I've found a 14-year-old girl who'd been kidnapped. She was still alive. Most had been dead."

Kay also sees ghosts.

"Sometimes I'll see them as wisps of smoke and sometimes as a complete human body that can be touched," she said. "I have some pictures of chimneys with orbs." Orbs, ghost experts say, are spirits that show up in photographs in the form of balls of light. "I contacted (the spirit of) my grandfather and asked why we were getting pictures of orbs around the chimney," she said. "He told me the chimney, because of the draft, worked as a portal."

Kay used to do psychic readings, but between hosting a radio show, personal businesses, speaking engagements, and working on a book, she just doesn't have the time. "I was told one time by a spirit that it wasn't really doing anybody any good," she said. "What I needed to do was teach people how to do it themselves. That's why I do the radio show."

But Kay warns people dabbling in the paranormal to tread lightly. You never know if you're going to step in something too deep. "Somebody like me, you have to stay focused and grounded in the real world," she said. "You can't let the paranormal things take over or you'll go crazy."

Kay organized the Quest Team, a group of paranormal investigators who've investigated thirty to thirty-five haunted places – such as Rotary Park in Independence. "My daughter and I used to take walks there almost every other night," Kay said. "After a while we both started noticing strange things. White balls of lights amongst the trees. We noticed a dark shadowy figure on the other side of the creek."

Kay and her daughter, also psychic, felt a "buzzing that just shook my jaw," Kay said. "We found a number of spirits there. One of them being a woman that haunts a tree." Kay said the spirit is a woman who taught in a schoolhouse that used to sit near the park. "I think (ghosts) travel to their old haunts, as you will," Kay said. "They will appear at places that they feel comfortable during their lifetime."

And in those places, Kay will find them.

10

Was There Once Life on Mars?

A face stares into the heavens. It's surrounded by long-silent ruins, keeping watch for a civilization millions of years dead. Somewhere on Earth? Try Mars.

Kansas City, Missouri, author Mac Tonnies thinks there's life on our nearest planetary neighbor. Maybe there's no longer intelligent life – as he postulates in his book, *After the Martian Apocalypse: Extraterrestrial Artifacts and the Case for Mars Exploration* – but he thinks life's there nonetheless, probably microbial, but there may be vague remnants of more complex life forms. "Carl Sagan finally said it is scientifically testable," Tonnies said about the late astronomer who was once a skeptic of extraterrestrial life. "That's where I'm coming from in the book."

Earthbound eyes have looked toward Mars for centuries. The ancient Greeks saw Mars with the naked eye, in the late 1800s Professor Percival Lowell thought he saw canals on the surface of Mars, and Orson

The late Mac Tonnies, author of *After the Martian Apocalypse: Extraterrestrial Artifacts and the Case for Mars Exploration.*

Welles scared the bejesus out of America in 1938 with his "War of the Worlds" broadcast.

In the mid-1970s, NASA sent the Viking probes to Mars in hopes of discovering life on the Red Planet. "Of the Viking tests, two of three tested positive," Tonnies said, noting with disdain that although the tests hinted at organic life, NASA disputed the results. "I think it's a given there's at least microbial life on Mars."

Tonnies, an author and graduate of Independence's William Chrisman High School and Ottawa University, has more than just a passing connection with the Red Planet. He was born August 20, 1975 – the day NASA launched the Viking Mission to Mars.

Tonnies is unimposing – tall, thin, bespectacled – until he speaks, throwing out head-scratching, multisyllabic words with the ease of a college pitcher striking out eighth graders. "I'm a writer first and foremost," he said. "That's what I do." Tonnies' first book was a collection of short stories, *Illumined Black and Other Adventures*, published in 1995 and still available on Amazon. com. "I consider myself a fiction writer," he said, but he's really interested in Mars.

An editor looking at Tonnies' fiction was also familiar with Tonnies' Martian website. So the editor pitched a book idea, and Tonnies agreed. "It was a very good publishing deal."

After the Martian Apocalypse scientifically explores anomalous structures on Mars, which probes have photographed multiple times. Structures with names like the "face," the "D&M pyramid" and the "city." From the photographs, these structures look symmetrical and suspiciously artificial. "It started with the face," Tonnies said of a human-like helmeted face – complete with two eyes, a nose and mouth – first photographed in 1976 staring into space from a region of Mars dubbed Cydonia. "NASA waved (the humanoid appearance) off as a trick of light and shadows. And that was it. But they took another picture."

That picture, taken from a different angle under different lighting conditions, showed the same thing – a giant humanoid face on the surface of Mars. NASA took another picture of the face in 1998. This picture – admittedly doctored by NASA, according to Tonnies – revealed an uneven, natural surface life-on-Mars enthusiasts dubbed "the cat box." That picture, according to NASA, proved the face was just a natural, windswept structure. The face crowd cried foul.

Tonnies and other proponents of life on Mars, such as the movement's poster child, Richard C. Hoagland, are convinced the scientific community is covering up the idea of intelligent life on our neighbor. "Tom Van Flanders (a Ph.D. who has spoken out on Martian life) has come to the conclusion that the face and other anomalies are indisputable evidence that there was life on Mars," he said.

The face, and other curious features in the Cydonia region, have been run through programs that search for man-made structures, Tonnies said. These same programs were used to pick hidden man-made items – such as vehicles – out of satellite images taken during the Gulf War. Because vehicles have a symmetrical structure, the computer determined the images were artificial. The results from the Mars analysis are that some of the structures on Mars are artificial, Tonnies said.

"The face has quantifiable features a computer can recognize. If we saw these things on Earth (from satellite) we'd immediately call in archeologists," Tonnies said. "It's just silly, bad science."

In 1976, NASA steered the Viking probes away from the Cydonia region, Tonnies said. "They were going to land the Viking in Cydonia," he said. "And they took a picture of the face and changed their minds. "NASA said the terrain is too bumpy. Then they land them in a field of boulders."

And in 2003, NASA again avoided the Cydonia region with the Spirit and Opportunity landers. This mission, still under way, was to determine if there was life on Mars. But the rovers weren't equipped to detect current life, they were equipped to help scientists study Martian geology. "The reason JPL (Jet Propulsion Laboratory, a branch of NASA in charge of Mars exploration) is averse to finding life, their study of Mars is purely geological," Tonnies said. "Steve Squires, the head of the rover team, was looking at (a picture of an) organic thing and he said 'it's driving me crazy. I can't explain it.' Well, maybe if you'd get out of your geologic module."

But maybe finding life on Mars won't be left up to JPL. The European Space Agency has also studied the Red Planet and has come up with some interesting findings. Such as methane, a fragile gas with a limited life span. Methane is created by either recent organic or volcanic activity – and scientists have never detected recent volcanic activity on Mars. ESA may have also detected another organic compound on Mars – ammonia. The results, however, are inconclusive.

Much like Bigfoot having primate expert Jane Goodall in its corner, the life-on-Mars believers have theirs. Arthur C. Clarke, a heavy-hitter in the science and science-fiction communities who invented satellite communication and wrote such books as *2001: A Space Odyssey* and *Childhood's End*, is convinced there's life on Mars. Clarke has dubbed Martian 3D vegetation-like structures that NASA has photographed growing and waning with the seasons "banyan trees." JPL has claimed what Clarke and others have seen is melting frost. "That's where JPL is being disingenuous. They're not talking about the banyan trees," Tonnies said. "The closest NASA has come to addressing the banyan trees is suggesting Arthur C. Clarke is a little bit eccentric. "I think we should listen to him."

If Tonnies is right and Mars not only once supported intelligent life, but even now supports some form of microbial or vegetative life, what happened to the Red Planet? More importantly, what happened to the intelligent life? "Mars was destroyed by a relatively sudden event," Tonnies said. "A planet exploding." A rocky planet exploding in the proximity of Mars would explain why one side of Mars was pummeled by meteors, why an asteroid belt exists between Mars and Jupiter, and why intelligent life there may have died.

"Mainstream science thinks of (change in) the solar system as very gradual, but it's warming to the idea of a geographical catastrophe on Mars is very sudden," he said. "We need to go to Mars and find out what happened and if it will happen here."

Then the face, the pyramid and other structures may be the last pieces of the Martian civilization ... Or maybe not. Tonnies thinks it's possible there was once a civilization right here that was technologically advanced enough to make the trip through space. "We're finding that there was once a seafaring culture that predated the Egyptians. So it could have been an earth culture," he said. "But it could also be an indigenous species on Mars."

Then, why is it a humanoid face?

"I think life on Earth was created by comets. I think we have extraterrestrial life on earth (not-of-this-earth microbes scientists have recently found living in the upper atmosphere). Dialogue between planets has been happening for years. We'll find out we're relatives." Whatever you think, never ask Tonnies if he "believes" there was once life on Mars. You may not like his answer. "I don' like that word 'belief,'" he said. "Once you believe in something, the part of your brain that believes atrophies."

Kansas City, Missouri-based author Mac Tonnies, on whom Chapters 10 and 30 are based, passed away October 22, 2009. The 34-year-old Independence, Missouri, native was found dead in his apartment of "natural causes." Mac, who blogged daily on his award-winning website Posthuman Blues, was best known for his first non-fiction book, *After the Martian Apocalypse*, which he considered "a speculative and generally well-received examination of extraterrestrial intelligence on the Red Planet." Mac was just weeks away from the deadline for his next non-fiction book manuscript, *The Cryptoterrestrials: Indigenous Humanoids and the Aliens Among Us*, published in 2010.

I met Mac in September 2004 while I was managing editor of *The X Entertainment Magazine* in Kansas City. We sat in Starbucks on the Plaza, swilling coffee like college students, and discussed Mars, the possibility of extraterrestrial life, flavored coffee vs. good, old-fashioned, grizzled-newsman black, and which was better, the movie *Blade Runner*, or the book on which it was based, Philip K. Dick's *Do Android's Dream of Electric Sheep?* He liked the movie; I liked the book. That was the only thing we disagreed on.

Over the next five years, I interviewed Mac for a number of newspaper and magazine articles, this book, and on the radio program "The Edge." Mac was a brilliant, original thinker in the esoteric field. He is greatly missed.

11

Does a Secret UFO Base Exist in Jefferson City, Missouri?

il McDonald, Sr., saw his first UFO in 1970. It wouldn't be his last. "I spotted one in the summer and it was almost over Carswell Air Force Base (in Fort Worth, Texas)," he said. "It was a huge one I labeled 'the mother ship.' It was very low and moving very slowly."

The ship, just entering the clouds, was metallic and cigar-shaped with a bulge in the middle. "This was a huge thing and it had several round openings in the hull," McDonald said. "Portals is what I called them. They may have been windows and they were heavily tinted. This thing was so low and so big I could see buff marks (on its surface). It was that close to me." McDonald called the base that Sunday afternoon and the Air Force spokesman said there had been no air traffic that day. "I'm sure that's what they would have said either way," he said.

McDonald served in the Air Force from 1958-64, then worked in law enforcement, the ministry, and served as a guard during the last ten years of the existence of the Missouri State Penitentiary in Jefferson City. And that's where his UFO encounters became overwhelming.

The prison that once held heavyweight champion Sonny Liston, was built in 1835 and was decommissioned in October 2004. *TIME* Magazine once called it 'the bloodiest 47 acres in America.' If McDonald's right, it may also be the most alien-infested 47 acres in America. McDonald said after his retirement, he's visited the area around the prison about once a month and has shot 112 minutes of infrared tape and has captured images of UFOs. "I had 20 pretty good ones on the film," he said. "I

Gil McDonald, Sr., is convinced there's a UFO base behind the walls of the old Missouri State Penitentiary in Jefferson City.

didn't see them, but got them on infrared film. One every seven minutes. That's a lot of traffic."

Before the prison was shut down in 2004, McDonald saw the first of many UFOs fly over Jefferson City and land at the prison. One night, McDonald was on the back side of the prison in Tower Ten when a disk he labeled the 'shuttle craft' landed in the yard. "I saw the shuttle craft dock in front of me," McDonald said. "But we didn't talk about stuff like that or would be fired immediately. We'd be mentally unfit for duty."

The ship was composed of two disks atop each other which were then topped by a dome. "Different parts of it were spinning in different directions except for the very top circle. It remained still," McDonald said. "It was obvious there was a force field around it. There was a tree limb inside the force field and the tree limb was spinning like in a wind storm but outside (the force field), everything, even the grass was still." He watched the device as it landed and took off again. "And then it didn't fly out, it just disappeared," he said. "But when it disappeared, it left a frozen image. It was there fifteen seconds and it just plopped to the ground like ice would."

Since, McDonald studies the night sky above Jefferson City. He's seen things there; things he's sure are not from our planet. "I've seen so many (UFOs) the last few years some people consider me a fake," he said. "It seems like any time I go out I'm going to get a picture of (a UFO) around Jefferson City."

But it's not the UFOs that have haunted McDonald – it's their occupants. "I saw a lot of those. I think they're from out of the cosmos," he said. "The best description I could give on those creatures is that they are the same thing we've always called ghosts. Some of them look like humans except they're gray; like they're drawn in pencil or something. Several times I have seen them walk directly through a solid object."

McDonald also saw alien executions, which made him think the Jefferson City Penitentiary was also a prison for them. "I did see them shoot a couple of their creatures and it wasn't like a laser gun," he said. "It looked like it shot something the size of a golf ball into them. The creature was shot and fell down and in two or three seconds it was dust."

But if anyone else saw UFOs or aliens at the penitentiary, they kept quiet about it. "They don't talk about them," McDonald said. "We had an inmate at one time who said he saw a ghost. They ridiculed him so bad he never said anything about it again. And

The penitentiary, built in 1835 and decommissioned in October 2004, was once called "the bloodiest 47 acres in America."

the officers knew they'd be fired if they brought it up."

So McDonald kept quiet, too. Then aliens began following McDonald when he left work. "It's like they go home with you," he said. "I don't really know what they're doing."

But whatever the aliens' purpose, McDonald said he doesn't think it's benevolent. He said he's seen evidence we may be lunch. "It makes me think that we're not on the top of the food chain," he said. "It looks like they're using humans. I think they take some people and don't bring them back. We should not trust them completely."

After McDonald retired, he decided not to keep quiet about the space alien presence in Jefferson City and launched his website (http://cosmostarman.tripod.com) to warn the world. "I'm just trying to give out information," McDonald said. "At first I was really excited about this, but it's got a real price tag attached to it."

McDonald said he's under government scrutiny. He's been followed and his telephone has been tapped. "I've been harassed for about three years now," McDonald said. "The entire neighborhood has been told I'm some kind of monster or totally insane. It drives people away from you. This is the authorities that are doing this."

He's even been paid a visit by the *Men in Black* (MIB); strange dark-suited, semi-human entities that have been reported harassing UFO witnesses since the modern UFO flap began in the 1940s. One night, while working bingo in Columbia, three MIB came into the room. "These three young guys come in. All were dressed in black suits," he said. "All were about the same size... Same kind of shirt, same kind of tie, same kind of haircut." Then they disappeared. McDonald asked, but no one remembered seeing them. "I'm just hanging out 100 percent and if the (government) wants to watch me or listen to me I'm not going to try to stop them," McDonald said. "I've been totally honest on this thing since the beginning and will continue to be."

McDonald hopes to see the day when his honesty is justified.

12

University of Missouri Professor Understands the Kalanoro

Under the surface of Madagascar, deep in the caves sacred to the Antakarana and Tsimihety peoples, lurk the Kalanoro. A recent Internet story alleges Navy SEALs photographed a group of thirteen Kalanoro in the late 1990s-early 2000s in the Democratic Republic of the Congo – far from the island of Madagascar. These Kalanoro were described as a gray "unidentified apes" with quills that run along their spines.

Legends of the Kalanoro are older than 1997 ... much older. The Kalanoro have been a part of Madagascar traditions since people arrived there 2,000 years ago. But opinions differ on what the Kalanoro might be.

According to travelafricamag.com, the Kalanoro is a physical creature covered with hair, less than three feet tall with long fingernails. One was reportedly captured by the Royal Geographical Society in 1889. The society discovered the Kalanoro not only had feet that point backward, the creatures were telepathic. In the 1964 volume *Western Folklore, Vol. XXIII*, an article by Bacil F. Kirtley – "Unknown Hominids and New World Legends" – paints the Kalanoro of Madagascar as a "land-dwarf" that, much like European elves and trolls, steals human children and replaces them with Kalanoro children.

University of Missouri-Columbia professor Joe Hobbs knows something about the Kalanoro, and their connection to children. While researching the relationship between people and caves in Madagascar, Hobbs came into contact, not with the Kalanoro, but with local people who are convinced the Kalanoro exist. "This story may strike some as funny," Hobbs wrote in a recent e-mail. "But the people in Madagascar are quite serious about these and other spiritual beings."

Unlike travelafricamag.com, Kirtley and the Navy SEALs story, the local people don't consider the Kalanoro to be animals – they are spiritual beings. In Hobbs' 2001 article, "People and Caves in Madagascar," published in The American Geographical Society's *Focus*, the people of Madagascar refer to the Kalanoro as "earth genies."

People of Madagascar who have historically buried their dead in caves have a great respect for the Kalanoro – because the Kalanoro physically interact with them. One Kalanoro near the village of Ambalakida, pays particular attention to bad parents, Hobbs said. "On three separate occasions, one as recently as 1998," Hobbs wrote in his 2001 article. "The being became angry that parents had insufficiently cooked meat for their children and done other things particularly unacceptable to it."

Unhappy with the parents, the Kalanoro kidnapped their children, Hobbs wrote. To get the children back, the distraught parents consulted another local spirit, a Tromba which had possessed a fellow villager. The tromba told the parents to leave offerings of honey and liquor in the forest. The parents did, the Kalanoro was pleased, and returned the children – one by one – to a local cave, the cave of Andoboara.

With permission from King Tsimiaro III, Hobbs visited the burial caves, including the cave of Andoboara, and saw first-hand the Kalanoro's influence on the local cultures. "The night we visited the cave, my assistant, Patty Vavizara, stayed close to me, fearful that the Kalanoro might be about," Hobbs wrote.

Regardless of whether the Kalanoro are real or legend, animal or intelligent and telepathic, unknown hominid or earth spirit; to the peoples of Madagascar, the Kalanoro are real.

13

The Night People

Young Vern often saw people outside his house at night. From age five to six, Vern would look out his bedroom window in Orrick, Missouri, and people with large, fishlike eyes would walk around his yard and sometime into his neighbor's houses. At the time, this wasn't strange to him. "They were the Night People," Vern said plainly. Everyone Vern knew – himself, his family, his friends – lived in the real world during the day. The people he saw outside his bedroom window lived there when the sun went down. "In my mind we were the Day People and they were the Night People. I know that sounds weird but that's how it seemed."

Vern, now an adult living in Liberty, Missouri, thought the Night People were normal. "I'd wake up at night and see these people with big eyes living a regular life," he said. "I could see faces, clothes, they had kids... I do remember the adult mowing the yard. But I thought it was weird because I couldn't hear the mower."

He also watched them walk up and down the street, pausing to speak with each other. "They seemed like they were talking and interacting normally," Vern said. "Like down home. You'd just see people talking."

Then Vern's family moved from Orrick to nearby Liberty and he saw the same fish-eyed Night People outside his window. One night, he finally made contact ... and never saw them again. "The children were playing in the yard next door and I thought, hey, I might go play with them," he said. "What's weird, though, is the last time I saw them, it seemed like all of a sudden they seemed to notice that I'd noticed them. One of the adults just looked at me and just realized, 'They see me now.' And the

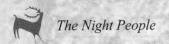

next thing I see is, it's daylight and I never see (them) again."
Vern had blacked out and came to hours later. "If this was real,
I probably wasn't perceived as a threat until I decided to come
out and play," Vern said.

But who were these Night People only Vern could see? Vern's
memories of them are similar to that of alien abductees who also
wake up to see large-eyed, friendly, familiar beings they later
identify as classic gray aliens.

Margie Kay, host of the Quest paranormal radio program,
ghost hunter, and psychic, said Vern's experiences were related
to alien abduction. "This is more common than most people
think," Kay said. "Vern is likely an abductee." Extraterrestrials,
Kay said, live in another dimension and are capable of entering and leaving ours whenever they want to – like Vern's Night
People.

Another piece of evidence may have come out of Vern's nose
when he was fourteen. "I had a nose bleed and didn't stop it,"
he said. "I finally blew my nose." What he found shouldn't have
been there. "It looked like a capsule of silvery something," he
said. "At first it felt hard then started dissolving. I was trying to
figure out what it was and it dissolved in my hand."

Many people who claim they've been abducted by extraterrestrials report similar metallic objects coming from their nose.
UFO researcher and physician, Dr. Roger Leir, has reported sur-
gically removing many similar objects from patients. "I wonder
if I wasn't tagged or something," Vern said.

Kay thinks he was. "This sounds like a typical implant in the
nose scenario," Kay said. "And he probably saw aliens, too."

Whatever the true origin of Vern's Night People – whether
they are the product of a child's imagination or alien abduction
– it's affected his life for decades. "You have to realize I was five
and six at the time," Vern said. "It's vivid enough I still remember it after 45 years."

14

The Man
Who Never Gets Cold

Whenever Harold Deal pulls into a parking lot in his adopted town of Greenwood, South Carolina, someone usually asks about his license plates. "I never get cold," he said. "So I have personalized license tags on my truck, 'NO COAT.' That's a conversation piece. That gives me the opportunity to share my experience with them."

"No Coat" Harold Deal stopped feeling cold when lighting struck him outside his Lawson home in 1969. *Photo courtesy of Harold Deal*

An electrical accident in 1969, that Deal no longer considers an accident, rendered him apparently impervious to cold. Since then, he spends his time counseling people who have experienced something similar.

Some experiences come from man-made electricity; Deal's experience came from the sky. The house, west of the small town of Lawson, Missouri, sat beneath a seething bank of thunderclouds the night of July 26, 1969, as Harold Deal, then 31, worked his second job as an electrical contractor under the rumble of thunder. Deal's ten-year-old son, Larry, who had accompanied him to the job, shook at every thunderclap. "My son begged me, 'Daddy, let's go home. Daddy, let's go home,'" Deal said. "I did."

Rain pounded the ground as Deal and his son ran from the house and into their pickup, lightning splitting the night sky. "It was raining really hard," Deal, now 73, said. "And lightning." Heavy raindrops splattered the windshield of Deal's truck as he drove to his nearby home at 102 Milwaukee Avenue in Lawson. "When I was about a block and a half from the house, I happened to look at my watch," Deal said. "It was 9:12 in the evening."

The next six hours were the fastest in Deal's life.

"I pulled into the driveway," he said. "It was lightning real bad." Deal, unprepared for the storm, had papers he didn't want to get wet, so he told Larry to run to the door to make sure it wasn't locked. "A lot of times my wife would be sewing in the basement and she'd lock the door," he said. "He ran up and opened the door and went in. That's when I started to get out of the truck." Deal grabbed his papers and stepped out. He took one quick step, two, three, and four – then his life exploded.

"Between the third and fourth step I felt like I was (riding) something real fast," he said. "It felt like my head was being sucked down between my shoulder blades." A bolt of lightning had struck Deal. His vision went white and he was thrown to the ground. "I felt like a pincushion was inside of me; every inch of my body," he said. "And I could not see. It was as though I stepped into a soft white cotton ball. I wasn't blinded. Everything was soft white around me."

Deal doesn't know if minutes or hours went by before someone spoke to him. "Next thing I knew I heard a voice," he said. "It was like I was under anesthesia. I thought I could make out the voices and I could answer them." But he didn't know who the voices belonged to and, although he couldn't feel anyone touch him, he knew someone helped him to his house. When he noted the time again it was 4:20 a.m. "I was out all night," Deal said. "I don't remember blacking out. But from that point on I didn't know anything. The initial hit was what I felt."

The lightning blast left two holes in Deal's driveway, one nineteen inches deep, one twenty three. The next morning the holes were full of water and nearby were what was left of Deal's boots. "There lay my bootlaces from my Army boots I bought that morning," he said. "They were still laced. It had pulled the eyes out."

For the next month Deal, who worked at the Trans World Airline overhaul base at Kansas City International Airport, couldn't use his feet or legs, and pain stabbed at his every movement. To relieve the pain, he underwent back surgery at St. Mary's Hospital in Kansas City, Missouri. "They ended up taking two vertebrae out of my back," Deal said. "I was about five feet, eight and a quarter inches and I ended up after surgery two and a quarter inches shorter." After surgery, the pain was gone, but doctors gave him a dire warning "When I was at St. Mary's they told me I'd never walk again," Deal said. "After I could get my breath, I asked the doctor, 'What are my odds?' He said, 'The bottom line is, after surgery, you either walk or you don't.'" After surgery, as Deal came out of anesthesia, his wife sitting at his bedside, he systematically moved his toes, then his feet, then his legs. "I could hear the nurse say, 'He's alright,'" Deal said. "I had to know whether I had control of these legs or not."

But the lightning strike changed his life in ways he couldn't fathom. Although he could now use his legs, he would often forget how to move them.

"One day I was in my front room and it took me about two and a half hours to get up out of the chair," Deal said. "I was physically able to, but it affects your nervous system so bad I couldn't remember what it took to get out of the chair. I was up town one day, I stopped to talk to a friend and it took me an hour and a half to remember what to do to get moving again."

But the most peculiar effect from the lightning strike is Deal's ability, or inability, to feel cold. "The way this lightning has left me, I never get cold," Deal said. "I've been out in seventy-two below zero temperature (in Hell, Michigan). I don't wear a jacket. I don't wear long sleeves, I don't wear long pants." Deal not only doesn't feel cold, his flesh seems impervious to it.

Mary Ann Cooper, MD, of the Lightning Injury Research Program at the University of Illinois at Chicago, said lightning

The Lawson Review
The Home of Watkins Woolen Mill State Historic Site

| Volume 112 | Number 40 | November 24, 1993 |

"No Coat" Deal is thankful he's able to share his experience

Call him "Weird Harold".

Call him "No Coat".

Call him if you've survived a lightning strike or a severe electrical shock because he understands what you're going through.

Not more than a handful of years ago, Harold Deal would change the subject when anyone mentioned his experience as a lightning strike victim. Now he travels to those obscure little places on the map to tell of his ordeal and to offer brief insights into the life of a lightning strike survivor.

Doctors still don't fully understand what happened to Harold's body after he was hit by lightning in July 1969. They will confirm that his is one of the most unusual cases they have ever come across.

Harold is unaffected by the cold or pain. His recovery from major and minor injuries is swifter than normal.

The doctors can't explain it and neither can Harold. After 24 years, Harold has learned to accept his uniqueness and he now shares his experience with other lightning strike and electric shock victims. Harold is a member and the Public Relations Director of the Lightning Strike and Electric Shock Victims, International.

His latest extraordinary medical diagnosis is with a bone cyst and a fractured left leg. Harold went to see the doctor because he was experiencing some discomfort in his leg. The doctors couldn't explain what happened but said if it had been anyone else, they would not have been able to walk with that type of cyst or fracture.

He attends the Lightning Strike and Electric Shock Victims, International conventions and has been featured on a national television program relating his experience as a lightning strike victim.

He spends hours and hours on the telephone talking with other victims, offering them comfort and assurance that they are not alone.

At this time last year, Harold was on his way to the Third Annual Lightning Strike and Electrical Shock Victims International Convention in Maggie Valley, North Carolina.

He stayed with Steve Marshburn, president of the group and during his visit with the Marshburns, Steve asked if Harold would be interested in talking with the school children there.

As Harold put it, "You know me. I never turn down the opportunity to talk about the group."

He has spoken with civic groups (large or small), 4-H Clubs, school clubs, and pre-school children.

"The Lord certainly blessed me being struck by lightning because he has brought me in contact with so many wonderful and very dear and special people," he said.

He shares what he went through, what worked and didn't work for him.

One of the biggest things he has been able to share with other victims is that fact that they are not going crazy and lightning affects every victim differently.

"Just like myself not getting cold in the winter time. As far as I know, I am the only person that is that way.

Harold says instead of feeling like an oddball or weirdo, victims have to realize that each person is affected differently and they just have to conduct as normal a life as they can.

It's difficult for survivors to explain what they've been through or what they are feeling because they don't understand it themselves.

Over the past year, Harold has talked with hundreds of lightning strike victims who have a variety of different problems.

He has talked to those who do not care to join the Lightning Strike and Electric Shock Victims, International group. They did not want to belong to any group that reminds them of their experience.

"I can certainly relate to that. I have told Steve so many times that the first eight years after I was struck by lightning, I would never have joined the group," Harold said.

On the other hand, there are those who learn of the group by coincidence and regard it as a lifesaver.

Coincidence? Harold doesn't think so. He feels victims are meant to come into contact with the group.

"I have never thought much about 'why I picked this time?' or wondered 'why am I going there?' because I know if it's meant for me to go, I will get on the flight.

Harold said the first time a person talks about their experience is the hardest. The second time is a little bit easier. And it gets easier each time after that.

It means a lot to Harold to be able to listen to their experiences and problems.

"To hear the ones talking, to hear the ones opening up and sharing their experiences, sharing their problems if you want to call it that. It makes them feel so much better from the simple standpoint that they are talking it out."

While attending a medical hearing concerning an electrical victim in Miami, Harold visited with the victim and her psychiatrist told Harold he could not believe the effect Harold's visit had on the victim.

Harold Deal has been featured in newspapers around the world – including his hometown Lawson Review. *Courtesy of Harold Deal* strikes could affect the body this way, but it's unpredictable. "His symptoms sound hypothalamic, but we cannot prove it nor do others have the same symptoms often," Cooper said. A hypothalamic dysfunction is the result of damage to the region of the brain that regulates many body functions.

"Most doctors tell me it's impossible," Deal said. "It's medically impossible. But medically they tell me I shouldn't be able to walk. I've said, 'Doc, you seen me walk in here didn't you? You're just using that 'medically' as an excuse.'"

Deal has been featured in the media across the world. He's been photographed sitting in a bathtub of ice and bathing in a snowdrift. He stood in only a pair of shorts for four hours in minus 70-degree temperatures for a television news program in Hell, Michigan. Heat bothers him, but pain, taste, and the sensation of cold are gone.

"Heat, when it gets around seventy degrees, it affects me as it would you like 120," he said. "When it gets around seventy-five to eighty degrees outside I pretty much stay in." During the summer, Deal said he often sits in a bathtub filled with water and six to eight bags of ice. "That's the only way I cool," he said.

Much like his resistance to frostbite, Deal has never sunburned.

But this path has been riddled with emotional trauma. Deal's first wife divorced him a few years after the lightning strike, and old friends in Lawson quickly disappeared. "I do not have physical pain," Deal said. "But if I had a choice I would take physical pain over psychological pain."

The emotional pain led to a night in 1991 when Deal considered suicide.

"I was tired of living," he said. "By the time you get one hurdle out of the way there's four more staring you in the face. I was just through with it. I was sitting in the chair with my hand on the phone bawling, hoping someone would call."

That's when Deal said God spoke to him. "He said, 'Harold, you feel you have to explain you're the way you are,'" Deal said. "He said, 'remember, there's two types of people out there. There's gossipers and there's sincere people. The sincere ones will ask you questions. The gossipers don't want the truth; they've got their mind made up. I don't know how to explain it. I just felt it." After that experience, Deal viewed his life from a different point of view. "Since I was struck by lightning I was thankful I was," he said. "I feel my life today is so much richer so much fuller. The Lord has shown me how to appreciate life. I don't take it for granted anymore."

This lead Deal to the group Lightning Strike and Electric Shock Survivors International, where he councils people who have also been struck by lightning. He met his second wife Sylvia through the group and moved to Greenwood, South Carolina, to marry her. She died from cancer in 2004. "I'm on the telephone an awful lot," Deal said of his work with electric shock victims. "I call into seven or eight states a week when I hear someone over there has been struck by lightning or electricity. I talk to them to give them psychologically what to expect."

Cooper respects Deal's work through his lightning strike group. "Harold has done a world of good for people and has a wonderful heart," she said.

But Deal's life isn't really about his life, or his inexplicable imperviousness to cold. It's about what he can do for other lightning strike victims. "It's not what Harold Deal has done, it's what the Lord has done through Harold Deal," he said. "Like I say, it's a big, big mystery. I can't explain it. All I can do is share it."

15

The Ghost of Dugan Lane

Dugan Lane runs north along Indian Creek through the wooded, hilly landscape of southern Missouri. It lies near a small town that boasted a tomato cannery during the Great Depression. The town is almost empty now, but this story isn't about the town, it's about a young woman who lived near the town at the turn of the 20th century.

Amanda Dawn is a fictitious name given to the young woman by Ozark author Ronnie Powell who promised family members and witnesses he'd never use real names, and, for the sake of Powell's pledge, the town's nameless, too. The house Amanda lived in isn't there anymore; it burned several years ago, but Powell knows Amanda's still there – he's talked with people who've seen her. "I've talked to people who say they actually saw the ghost of Dugan Lane," Powell said. "Two or three of the last surviving people who witnessed the ghost – they're dead now – and to them it was real. The ghost of Dugan Lane has some legend and truth in it."

Amanda lived in a house at the bottom of a hill with her husband and toddler, Roberta. One morning, Amanda sat Roberta on the floor and started preparing breakfast. When she turned to look for Roberta, Roberta was gone. "Roberta got curious," Powell said. "She tried to pick up a cricket and it hopped out the door and she went with it." Roberta wandered into the well house and fell into the well. "Amanda heard her scream and ran looking for her," Powell said. "The only thing she saw was Roberta's hand disappearing in the dark water below. They tried for days and days to find the body and never did."

Depression consumed Amanda. She sat staring at nothing for days. "A few days later she walked out to the road as her husband went to the corn field. Then went and jumped into the well," Powell said. "They found her body." For years after the tragedy, people saw Amanda walking the road crying out for Roberta. "The last time she's been sighted, strangely, was about a year ago," Powell said. "There's no house there or nothing, but this woman said she saw a woman dressed in an old tattered gown with long black hair. She didn't know anything of this story."

Powell stayed in the old house one night, waiting and watching for Amanda's ghost, but she never appeared. "There are areas and there are buildings that have very (strange) activities," he said. "I'm not afraid of ghosts and would like to see one and visit it. I'm on the upper end of non-believing, but there are things that are unexplained."

Powell's had an interest in ghosts, and writing, all his life – he's written six books and published two. His account of the ghost of Dugan Lane was published in the premiere issue of *Country Folk Magazine*.

As the years, and decades slip past, and people forget the story of Amanda and Roberta, a silent witness keeps vigil on Dugan Lane. "Whatever happens down there keeps happening," Powell said. "She's still looking for her little girl."

Powell's book, *South Through Bare Foot Pass*, is available in some local Ozark stores or by e-mailing him at captredoak@ todays-tech.com. His second book, *Tiddleson Son of Tiddle* – an Ozark fantasy adventure – will be available soon.

16

What's it Like to Live Without Fear?

*E*ighteen-year-old Ralph Carnahan was sitting on his family's porch in the southeast Missouri town of Zalma at about 9 p.m., May 7, talking to his girlfriend on the telephone, when he saw strange lights. "In front of me was a pair of bright lights in the sky; one light was red and one was white," he said. "The other pair off to my side, both were white."

He called his mother and her boyfriend outside. They didn't think the lights were out of the ordinary, so they went back in the house. Carnahan didn't; he waited and the lights moved closer. "The pair that was in front of me started hovering real slow and there's a tree in my front yard, it hovered around that tree," he said. Then the light moved off – but it left something behind. "There's a street light down the road and it glared on the tree. I looked up and there was something in that tree."

Carnahan saw a brownish-green creature with "real big eyes" sitting in the tree. He ran to the house and called his mother and her boyfriend outside again. "They came out and we tried to see what it was, but when we got close to it, I could see that (thing) started blending in with the tree," he said. "My mom didn't see it, so after a minute they went back in."

Carnahan walked to the porch where his mother's dog was tied; the dog soon started growling toward a bridge over a nearby creek. "I looked down by the Huzzah Creek by the bridge and there was a green spaceship not real big hovering as high as the street light, you could barely see it," he said. "I walked down to the bridge and checked it out. You could see it hovering backwards into the dark, so I turned around and … ran to my house."

From the front porch, Carnahan resumed talking to his girlfriend on the telephone. He told her everything he was seeing. "The alien in the tree was just staring straight at me, so my girlfriend said, 'Throw a rock at it or poke it with a stick,'" he said. "But I was on a phone with a cord and couldn't go very far with it, so I grabbed this coffee cup on the porch and threw it at it."

He missed the thing in the tree, but his action caused it to move. "I could hear the grass go down like something jumped on it," he said. "So I told my girlfriend that I'm going inside."

Carnahan went inside around 11 p.m. At 12:30 a.m., things in the house started to move; a tablecloth, a radio, a piggy bank, and sandals slowly shifted as if they were being inspected by a curious child. Carnahan was convinced aliens were in his house. "I knew it was aliens," he said. "But they were transparent; I could barely see them."

At about 5 a.m., Carnahan decided he didn't want to be alone. "A tall alien was looking through the glass on the top of the door," Carnahan said. "It was staring hard. It didn't have huge eyes and it was red with black markings on its face. He was scary." Carnahan woke his 16-year-old sister, "and I told her, 'look at the alien in the window,'" he said. "She started crying and ran into my mom's room." At dawn, Carnahan said the creatures disappeared.

"Mom didn't see them," he said. "She doesn't believe me or my sister, but I know different. They are out there and real. I'm not scared of anything, but now it's hard for me to go outside at night. "It ain't no joke," Carnahan said. "Aliens exist, one hundred percent."

17

Followed by the Unknown

The old house in Springfield was quiet, for the most part. Kerry Yates lived in the house for three years with various college roommates before something in the house decided to make itself known. "One night my girlfriend and I were in my bedroom with the CD player on listening to music and talking," Yates said. "The CD player quit playing music and we noticed a faint voice."

It was Friday in the fall, and Yates thought he was hearing the play-by-play announcer from the nearby high school football stadium. But the voice wasn't coming from the football stadium – Yates stuck his head out the window and listened. "Seconds later we heard it again," he said. "It was coming from the speaker on my CD player; the CD was not playing." Yates and his girlfriend Mindie listened to the speakers. The voice was male, but they couldn't make out what it was saying. "It was almost like you could hear about every third word then just mumbles," Yates said. "Eventually, I found myself talking to the speaker because it would only respond if we talked into it."

After about twenty minutes of this, the voice gradually got louder and seemed to get frustrated. "It was almost like he was getting mad that I couldn't understand him," Yates said. "He very clearly started saying 'God, God,' then continued mumbling. Then I started to get a little freaked out."

Things were quiet for a few minutes before Yates left the room and called his roommate. The voice didn't like that. "As I'm on the phone with him in the kitchen, the voice yelled, 'What the (expletive) does he want?'" Yates said. "I ran out of the house and so did my girlfriend."

The voice didn't return for two days, but this only marked the first of many strange occurrences for Yates. "From that point on, that seemed to open them up. It seemed like each house I went to, more things happened," he said. "Since that radio incident, it would just come on by itself. Things would get moved in my house a lot; just weird things all the time."

The house quickly gained a haunted reputation around school, and Yates had a hard time keeping roommates. So he moved; but no matter where he went, the voice moved with him. "My girlfriend was there when it started talking again," he said. "I asked, 'are you back?' It mumbled something and I said, 'are you back?'" Yes, it was back. "He said, 'I'm fixin' to leave; I'll be back in fifteen,' clear as a bell," Yates said. "The rest was just mumbles."

Yates and Mindie have moved out of Springfield to a new house in Buffalo, Missouri, and things are peaceful – almost. "We bought this new home and it never even crossed our minds something would happen, but then things started happening," he said.

Since they moved into the house, the TV turns on and off, noises thump in parts of the house, personal items appear in strange spots, and toilet paper disappears from the roll – which has caused more than one argument. But this house feels different.

"One night, I baked some cookies," Yates said. "I put them in a metal dish with a plastic lid and sat them on the counter. We got home at midnight and there's three cookies lying out of the pan and one had a bite out of it. A little bite, not like a grown person's bite. We kind of get the vibe that it's a little girl." And Yates's heard her. "I've heard a woman's or a girl's voice talking," he said. "I thought maybe the radio or TV was on, but there was nothing on. I woke Mindie up and she got scared."

Although Yates occasionally felt uncomfortable in the first house – like someone was watching him – he feels comfortable here. "I don't feel anything evil," he said. "I've always gotten positive vibes from this new house. The old house … there was some spookiness to it." Yates still owns the CD player, although he's happy he no longer hears the voice through it. "At first, when something like that happens, your first reaction is, oh, it's a ghost, ha, ha, just joking around. Then it got serious," Yates said. "At one point I was like, I'm done. I'm not messing with it any more."

18

A Light in the Woods

Dead leaves covered the forest floor. Young firs fought for sunlight among the tall, straight trees of Southeast Missouri. A small camper sat beside wood stacked for a campfire. Chris Black, of Park Hills, Missouri, rustled through the leaves on his property setting up a digital camera to capture photographs of deer; the next day was deer season.

Black usually slept in the camper during deer and turkey season, and did again on November 19, 2006. But the eve of this deer season was different. "Something kind of weird happened on my property," Black said.

Black set up the motion-activated camera at 2 p.m. – according to the time-stamped photo with Black's head in the foreground – and spent the rest of the afternoon getting ready for the first day of hunting season. "I was down there by myself," he said. "I'd sit by the fire and drink and one particular night, I got fairly (drunk), but I was sure of what was going on. I had a pretty big rip-roaring fire. As I sat there by the fire, I felt there was something else there. I remember feeling something there."

As Black sat before the fire drinking beer, he said into the night, "If anyone wants to come join me by the fire, you're more than welcome." He thinks something took him up on his offer. "Maybe that night at the property, I wonder if I didn't invite something," he said. "I just kinda got mesmerized by the fire. That's when I felt something there."

After a time, Black put out the fire and went to bed. But the feeling of his visitor grew unnerving. "The door to the camper can only be locked on the inside," Black said. "I woke up at 3 or 4 in the morning and the door wouldn't open like it was locked. It was stuck hard. I kicked on it, I beat on it, I couldn't get it open.

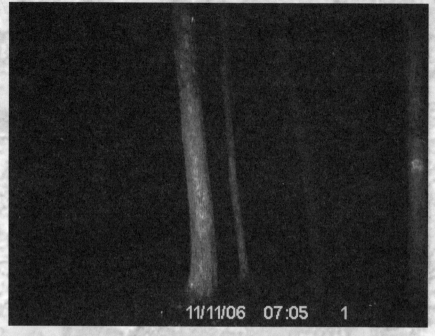

11/11/06   07:05   1

A picture from the trail camera of deer hunter Chris Black, of Park Hills.
Photo courtesy of Chris Black

I started to panic." Black thought the door had been barred from the outside. "It was a camper door and I should have been able to kick right through it," he said.

Thinking someone was outside, he grabbed his shotgun and yelled a warning that he was going to shoot at the door. "It would not budge," Black said. "I shot a hole completely through where the lock is and the door still wouldn't open. After I shot about half a dozen holes in the door I kicked the handle through the door and then I hit it with my shoulder and it came open. There was absolutely no way it would have been locked."

No one was outside the camper, nor was there evidence the camper door had been barred. The rest of the night was quiet, but this wasn't the last strange encounter he'd have relating to that property or that deer season. The trail camera had captured something anomalous. The motion-activated camera had shot a picture of a deer, but it also captured two lights that should not have been in the woods, far away from roads. "One of them, the round one, you can tell it's moving straight up from the ground," he said. "It's round and I swear it almost looks like you can make

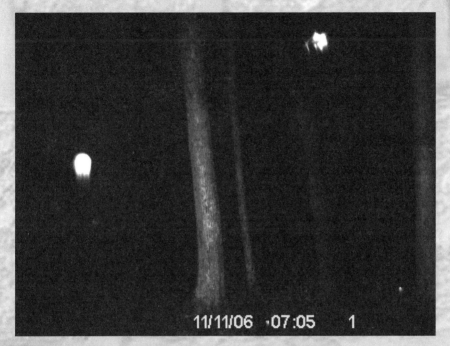

11/11/06 ·07:05   1

A picture taken seconds later – miles away from any homes or roadways. Chris Black has no idea what could have caused those lights. *Photo courtesy of Chris Black*

out a face in it. The other one in the upper right hand corner is moving from right to left in an upward angle. It looks like a star shape. You can see edges on it."

These strange lights corresponded with his visitor ... and his panic in the camper. "I've seen stuff I haven't been able to explain and I know there's not an explanation. I know there's things out there."

And, after this night of terror, Black thinks it followed him home. "I have some unreal activity going on around me," Black said. "Doors move when I walk past. Not just at home, but everywhere; at work, home, Walmart. I see it everywhere. I almost feel like something is following me."

Black said his invitation, "if anyone wants to come join me by the fire, you're more than welcome," seemed to bring something to him as if he had used a Ouija board – something Black has always been too cautious to use. "I've seen them (Ouija) but I've never touched them. I've never messed with them," he said. "I'm scared to death to touch one. I didn't want to invite something in my house you can't get rid of." Black's campsite visitor is just that – something he can't get rid of.

He first felt the visitor in November 2006 and doors around him began moving on their own soon after. "It's kind of like (the door) follows me when the door's already open," he said. "It doesn't just move one way; it'll move about four inches when I walk by it either way. It's almost like something's pulling it to me when I walk to it and pushes it away when I go past."

Black first started noticing this phenomenon at his home in February or March. "When you first go in the house there's a metal door, and the next door is a wooden door. It moves every time I walk past it," he said. "My bedroom door is a wooden door. It's never done it before but it moves now every time I go past it."

At first, Black tried to find a terrestrial explanation for the moving doors – movement of air, the doors weren't level, even the building shifting. "I've even thought the weight of my body might shift it a little bit, but it happens to doors set on concrete floors," he said. "I'm trying to debunk this thing anyway I can but I don't understand. Do I have something following me around that I can't see and nobody else can see? This is really, really weird crap."

And it's not just Black who sees the doors move. Family members and coworkers have all seen it occur. "I've even had my dad watch and witness it and a guy at work," Black said. "There's a door to the break room going to the outside area where we smoke. He was right behind me. We walked by the entry door and I heard a creak and the door moved six inches." Black asked his coworker if he'd seen the door move; he hadn't. "Then I backed up and went through it again and he said, 'That's some weird (stuff),'" Black said. "There's weird crap that happens to me all the time; it's almost like things happen so often that I don't pay attention to it anymore."

So far, Black hasn't experienced anything negative from his visitor, but is worried the occurrences will escalate to something unpleasant. "I really haven't noticed anything angry or malevolent," Black said. "It hasn't caused any harm like that to me. It's just something weird that happens and it's happening more and more."

19

1973 was a Busy Year for UFOs in Missouri

*N*ineteen seventy-three was a busy year for Missouri. The Worlds of Fun amusement park opened, the Kansas City Royals played its first year in a new ballpark, and a major fire destroyed more than eighty percent of the U.S. Army and U.S. Air Force records stored in a St. Louis warehouse. These events may have kept most Missourians' eyes from the skies, but not everyone's – 1973 was also a busy year for UFOs.

UFO investigator Dr. Harley Rutledge, a former physics professor at Southeast Missouri State University, investigated a string of UFO reports that began that year on February 21, in Piedmont, Missouri. That work later led to his book, *Project Identification: The First Scientific Field Study of UFO Phenomena.*

Many people from Piedmont – including police officers – reported their cars stalled when a light sped above them. When television signals scrambled, many TV watchers walked outside to see similar lights moving overhead, according to Rutledge's book.

Those would be just the first of a rash of UFO reports from at least twenty Missouri communities in 1973.

A woman in Charleston, Missouri, saw an egg-shaped object flying just above the trees near her home. Multiple witnesses near Elsinore, Missouri, reported strange hovering lights. A dish-shaped object a witness claimed had landing gear and portholes, landed in the woods near Ellsinore. Ted Phillips, a Missouri UFO investigator, found scorched ground and damaged foliage there, leading him to the conclusion that, yes, something had landed. Strange lights were also seen by pilots over Farmington, and again over Piedmont.

Law enforcement officials reported seeing numerous UFOs near Dexter, Missouri. Gray and blue cylinder-shaped UFOs were seen near Springfield and Cape Girardeau that summer. A veterinary technician at the University of Missouri witnessed dogs reacting to an egg-shaped object seen early one morning flying over Emden, Missouri.

In October, a trucker near Jackson, Missouri, claimed he was injured by a passing UFO, and in November, a woman reported being chased by a humming UFO near Matthews, Missouri. The object trailed her until she finally pulled off the road only to see it shoot overhead.

But the biggest UFO news might not be the rash of credible reports by citizens, law enforcement officials, and pilots. The biggest news might be the aforementioned St. Louis fire that destroyed Army and Air Force records.

During an investigation of a possible 1941 UFO crash near Sikeston, Missouri, a local researcher discovered *all* the records of the Missouri Institute of Aeronautics, which responded to the crash, burned in that fire (for more on that story, see Chapter 2). Conspiracy or coincidence?

Although many Missourians have reported seeing UFOs over the decades, the frequency, the detail, and the importance have yet to equal the sightings of 1973.

20

Screams of the Alien

Scott Palmer's family moved from Chicago to Marceline, Missouri – population 2,650 – in 1981. His parents wanted to raise their family somewhere small and safe. Eleven years later, he experienced something that was neither small nor safe. "I feel I ran into some people from another planet," he said.

Palmer was twenty-one years old in 1992 when he and friend Jim Rauer moved to Columbia, Missouri, to work. Palmer's sister, Stephanie, was attending the University of Missouri-Columbia at the time and let them live with her for a few weeks until they could afford an apartment. "She had moved out of a sorority house and moved in with some roommates," he said. Her three roommates were sorority sisters. "My friend and I, we moved up there because we thought it would be a good place to party it up."

They soon discovered it wasn't.

"One of my sister's roommates was a blonde-haired, blue-eyed girl. Very pale skin," Palmer said. "I kind of took a liking to her." The girl, about 5'8" and muscular "like a gymnast," Palmer said, was intelligent and quiet. Rauer said there was something strange about the way she looked. "She certainly didn't look normal," he said. "She had really blonde hair, she was pale and she was homely as all get out."

But the way the girl looked, Palmer and Rauer soon discovered, wasn't the only strange thing about her. Although Rauer said she was shy, he also said she "didn't have a clue about normal life."

"Sometimes you would ask her questions and she'd just look like she wasn't sure what you were talking about," Palmer said. "Like 'who won the World Series?' 'Hey you remember the Rubik's Cube?' Stuff everyone should know. I thought, 'Where's she from?'"

As the relationship progressed, so did the aura of strangeness. "I ended up having a sexual relationship with her," Palmer said. "On her part it was emotionless. She acted like she didn't know what to do. But I was still interested in her."

Soon after, Palmer discovered the girl had a boyfriend. He was blonde, like her, and also like her, there was something not quite right about him. "He came over a few times and never showed any aggression towards me," Palmer said. "I thought when I heard he was coming over we would probably get into it but he never even showed me any kind of response. Like he didn't care." The only thing strange about the boyfriend, Rauer said, was the way he looked. "I do remember thinking he was way better looking for a guy than she was better to pull," he said. "But I only saw them two to four times max."

The "boyfriend" didn't visit often, and the girl didn't talk about him, so Palmer pursued the relationship. A few weeks later, the girl's sister came for the weekend. That's when things changed for Palmer and Rauer. "Her sister looked a lot like she did," Palmer said. "They were sisters, but it was really weird. They were the same height, and so on. They were in very good condition. I remember how clean and clear their skin was. They were like twins, but they weren't twins." Rauer isn't convinced they weren't. "They looked so much alike they looked like twins," he said.

Palmer suggested a double date. While he and Rauer sat on the couch watching TV as they waited for the sisters to get ready, something happened that left both men terrified. "We're waiting around for them," he said. "They're sitting behind us talking. We're not thinking anything about it; then they got into a little bit of an argument."

The sisters moved to another room as the argument got louder – then Palmer and Rauer heard something that froze them to the couch. "All of a sudden it just got really loud," he said. "Right as we were thinking about getting up and investigating, we heard their language switch over."

Noises, high-pitched and crackling, came from the girls in the other room.

"What we heard was something out of a *Star Wars* movie," Palmer said. "If it was a language, which I'm sure it was because they were speaking to each other; it sounded like insects or something." Palmer and Rauer sat in front of the TV, unable to move. "The two sisters got into it," Rauer said. "They were speaking perfectly normal English, then when they got heated, it was something I've never heard, never heard before and I'm sure I'll never hear again. There's no good way to describe the sounds that came out of their mouths."

The young men could only sit on the couch as the girls argued in the other room. "We looked at each other," Rauer said. "As soon as we looked at each other when it went to the clicks and squeals it was like, 'Scott, door, now.'" Palmer said the two were still too shocked to move. "Our bodies just shut down," he said. "I'm not sure how much time went by but I remember getting myself together and walking out on the balcony. I just stood there and I just couldn't think. I was still in shock. I was just trying to catch my breath."

A few minutes later, Rauer met him on the balcony. "My heart was beating fast, I couldn't breathe well," Palmer said. "I looked over to him and asked, 'Did you just hear what I heard?' He said, 'Let's go for a walk.'" The young men walked out of the apartment to a nearby sand volleyball pit. "I don't know who those girls are," Palmer remembers Rauer saying. "But they're not from this planet."

For a time Palmer tried to reproduce the sounds, but the clicks and squeals escaped him. "To this day I can't reproduce those sounds," Palmer said. "It was too otherworldly." Rauer couldn't mimic the noises either. "I don't think he or I could ever reproduce that," Rauer said. "It was absolutely the strangest noises I've ever heard."

Then the thought hit them – they'd heard something they weren't supposed to hear. "We were smart enough to say whatever that was, they don't want to be known," Palmer said. "We decided to go back in (the apartment) because we didn't want to alarm them. We might be in maximum danger."

When they returned to the apartment, the sisters were sitting quietly on the couch. "I can't remember how it went down, but they said 'Where did you go?'" Palmer said. "I'm not sure what our answer was. I think we hung out with them a little bit, but I don't remember any detail after that." Rauer's memory after that point is just as sketchy.

"The rest of that evening was a blank," Rauer said. So is his memory of the girls' names. "I sure don't remember, and that's awfully funny because I've never forgotten anyone I've ever met and I can't remember their names. If we could find what their names were, if they were gone and there was no trace of them, that would convince me that something strange was going on."

After that day, the story remained between the two until 2007 when Palmer told his sister. "She's a real straight shooter, real conservative," he said. "When I told her that story she said, 'Wow. I always thought something was strange. Something about that girl that didn't make any sense.' That was out of character for her." If she remembered the girls' names, she wouldn't disclose it.

Palmer is convinced the sisters were the "Nordics" of UFO lore. UFO researchers claim the Nordics – called such because of their resemblance to Scandinavians – are an alien race that look similar to average humans, but are slightly taller, in excellent physical condition, with pale skin, blue eyes and blonde hair, according to Marilyn Ruben of www.abduct.com. The high-pitched clicking sounds and lack of emotion, she said, are common. The sex, however, is not. "There's no doubt in my mind that those girls were from a different planet," Palmer said. "It was a life-altering thing."

Although the encounter terrified Rauer, he's not as convinced as Palmer the sisters are from anywhere but here. "In no way shape or form am I convinced of that," he said. "I couldn't count it out, but the chance of them being extraterrestrial is about 1 billion to one. But (Palmer) is absolutely convinced."

Alien abduction researcher and writer Donald Worley (www.abduct.com) agrees with Palmer's conviction that the girls were from another planet, but doesn't think they were Nordics. "These non-twins are most likely some kind of halflings (alien-human hybrids)," he said. "Their behavior and descriptions are more similar to halflings and not the Nordics."

Rauer places the behavior of the girls in a more terrestrial setting – twin speak. "I remember looking up on the Internet about twin speak that sounded like what I'd heard," he said. "Humans have done some strange things." Regardless, the experience has haunted him for years. "I've come across a grizzly bear in Alaska," he said. "And nothing has scared me like that."

21

Strange Visitations are Common at The Parlor

*T*he doorbells of The Parlor Bed and Breakfast in Ironton, Missouri, ring at odd times. Jeannette Schrum, co-owner of the bed and breakfast since 2000, is used to it. It's probably ghosts. Flying curtains, falling clocks and strange shadows on the walls are common occurrences in the bed and breakfast that, for a short time in the 1960s, was a funeral parlor. But Schrum said there has been unexplained activity in the home much longer than that.

"The place had been haunted since the '20s and '30s, as far as we can trace back," she said. "When we bought the place, they told us it was haunted and I said 'bull.' I really don't believe in that sort of thing." Schrum purchased the building with her husband, Robert Halket, Mayor of Ironton, and her sister and brother-in-law, Dana and Moody Campbell.

Architect Charles J. Tual built the home between 1901 and 1908 for him and his wife, the exterior constructed of concrete blocks made on site. A mortician purchased the home in 1960 and turned it into a funeral home. Although the building served in that capacity for only a short time, that time has a close connection to Schrum. "My great grandfather was one of the few bodies that was laid out here when it was a funeral parlor," she said. "And my grandmother worked here." And she may still be there. Although Schrum, who was raised not to believe in the paranormal, said the spirit of "a lady" – possibly her grandmother – follows her around the house. "I have a woman friend," she said. "It's something you just know it's there. It's a woman and it's always a warm, friendly feeling. My grandmother and sister and I were all very close. I'd like to think it's her, but I'm a non-believer."

Even to a non-believer, too many unexplainable events happen in the bed and breakfast. The new owners began renovating the home when they bought it in August of 2000 and immediately noticed something wasn't right. "When we first started working on it, things would disappear," she said. "I kept it to myself because I knew the guys were going to make fun of me."

By that time, Schrum had met her lady. Then her family began experiencing things, too. On a hot night, Schrum went to the porch to check on guests who sat talking in the evening breeze, when her sister called to her. "She was standing with her back to the kitchen and pretty soon my sister's at the door saying, 'come here, come here,'" Schrum said. "She said, 'Did you walk up behind me a few minutes ago?' I said, 'She got you, she got you, she tagged you, she got you.'"

Schrum could talk about it now; someone else had experienced her lady. Some time later, her husband received a more formal introduction. "He was reared back in the recliner and had a pizza in one hand, a Diet Pepsi in the other," Schrum said, "and he said, 'Oh my God. She just walked across there, stopped and looked at me, and kept on walking.'" The woman Halket saw wore a long, gray period dress, her hair pulled up in a bun on the back of her head. "My husband hates it," she said. "He just hates it."

Voices whisper in the night at The Parlor and when people turn to see who's there – no one ever is. Guests see a smiling little boy playing in the main parlor, and a man wearing a white shirt standing in a window. But the most common activity at The Parlor are shadows. Shadows of people often walk the porch of The Parlor, and sometimes wander the interior of the building. "I see shadows all the time," Schrum said. "The shadows are just unbelievable. They're day and night both."

Belinda Clark-Ache, founder of Haunted Missouri Paranormal Studies, has investigated The Parlor and knows the bed and breakfast is haunted. When her paranormal team stayed there, members felt dramatic changes in temperature; taps on the shoulder and one man heard someone whisper his name – even though he was alone in the room. "We were woken up at 5:30 a.m. hearing our names called in the hallway," Clark-Ache said, going through the experiences of the evening. "Two different doors on the second floor hallway opened at the same time. There was the smell of fresh bread baking – she didn't make us fresh bread that weekend." The most compelling evidence she saw was in a room called, "The Brass Bed."

Tim Harte MA, LCPC, University if Illinois-Springfield, was with Haunted Missouri Paranormal Studies that night, and had set up in The Brass Bed a computer system he developed with Dave Black, also of the university, that is designed to measure energy frequencies associated with haunt phenomena. Included was an infrared video camera with microphones. "When he turned in for the night, he left the machine recording," Clark-Ache said. "About twenty minutes later, you hear what sounds like him coming through the room. Then the bathroom light comes on. You hear bathwater and splashing. You hear draining and the bathroom light goes off. The rest of the recording is silent."

No one took a bath in that room, or slept there during the investigation – and no one was visible on the video. "Anyone going from the bedroom to the bathroom would have been discernable on the tape," she said. "We could not reproduce the event. That's got to be the most excited I've ever been about a piece of evidence and it wasn't even mine."

Although Schrum doesn't embrace the ghosts of The Parlor, she doesn't want to hide the fact that the home is haunted. "I've had couples get up in the middle of the night and leave," she said. "I put (the haunting) on the website because I didn't want anyone to come in here and be frightened. That's not fair. That's not what they bargained for."

22

Strange Things Over Kansas City, Missouri

*T*here are things in the sky – unidentified things. Some hovering, some flying, some triangular, some round. The Mutual UFO Network takes hundreds of reports of UFOs each month. But maybe the strange part of these reports isn't the people who see Unidentified Flying Objects; it's the people who don't see them.

Janice Vaughan of Des Moines, Iowa, was a Kansas City, Missouri, teenager in 1986 when she and her mother were driving to the mall. "We stopped at a red light," Vaughan said. "Glancing out my window on the passenger side, I saw a huge silver disc with lights rotating around the middle hovering above the building on the northwest corner of Antioch and Englewood Road." The disc dwarfed the buildings at this busy intersection. It just hung there silently. "I said something like, 'Mom, look,'" she said. "We were both stunned by what we were seeing."

While they watched, the object glided silently over the road and briefly hovered over a movie theater. "Then it whooshed off to the west and disappeared from our sight behind some houses," Vaughan said. "We turned right onto Englewood Road, abandoning our original errand, and drove around the neighborhoods hoping to see it again, but we didn't find it." Then Vaughan and her mother drove home. "We told my step-dad about it and watched the news that night for any mention of it," she said.

But there were no news reports on the UFO that night or in the newspaper the next day. Vaughan doesn't understand how no one else saw the object, but she knows she did. "It was the most incredible thing I've ever seen," she said. "If my mom hadn't been with me I think I would have convinced myself by now that it didn't really happen. Once in a while my mom and I will talk about it again, and I'll ask her to tell me what she remembers about that day, just to verify my memories of it."

Jim Johnson, Kansas City Section Director for the Mutual UFO Network said this type of sighting – a singular witness over a busy area – is all too common.

"Many of the reports I have received over the last decade-and-a-half with MUFON are from high-traffic areas," Johnson said. "I was able to get to one of the scenes within an hour or so of the sighting event." The witness of this 1997 event, Johnson said, was convincing. "Whatever she saw, she wasn't making it up," Johnson said. "(She) took me back to the locations where she turned off at Southwest Trafficway at 34th Street (another busy intersection) traveling north."

The oblong object, roughly shaped like a rugby ball, moved slowly over a television tower then toward a second television tower about a mile away before it "blinked out." "It lasted a couple minutes," Johnson said. "Her impression was that others were seeing it as well, as cars were slowing down and pulling to the right lane, but she was the only one who stopped." Like the other UFO sighting, there were no news reports about it the next day. So, why is it no one else saw these UFOs moving slowly over busy streets in the middle of the day?

"I have come to believe that in many cases, the people who are supposed to see flying objects, see them repeatedly, and the rest of us see them rarely, if at all," Johnson said. "Keep in mind that most people aren't looking for them and don't want to get involved even if they do see them. The rest of us keep looking up."

23

Mom's Ghost is Still Watching

As Alzheimer's disease slowly deconstructed the mind of Denise Gedlund's mother, she forgot her family – everyone but Denise. Denise was her mother's youngest child, and that may have been why. "I come from a large family of two boys and three girls, of which I am the baby," she said. "All my sibs grew up almost a generation before me and I was like an only child."

Denise's mother was diagnosed with Alzheimer's in 2005 and died in February 2008. "Much of the upsetting details of her last few months in life were kept from me by the family, for which I am grateful," she said. "I was very, very close with my mother. The past three years were very difficult for the family." During the last few times Denise saw her mother, she didn't know Denise's name, but knew who she was. "She knew that I was her baby girl," Denise said. "In fact, for a long time I was the only person she recognized."

As Denise and her siblings watched their mother fade from life, they sometimes saw flashes of her old self. "To the last my mother had a great and wicked sense of humor," Denise said. "Even two days before her death she was teasing the nurses to bring her booze with her ice water."

Denise's mother died at 6 a.m. February 1, 2008. "I am still having difficulty," Denise said.

But Denise soon found her mother isn't really gone because she comes to visit. "About a week after her passing I was lying in bed reading when I heard footsteps come into the room and felt a heavy weight sit on the end of the bed," she said. "I thought it was my boyfriend but when I looked he was not there, but I did see a definite butt print on the sheets."

However, she wasn't afraid because she knew who had visited her. After several similar visitations, Denise began calling out, "Mom's here."

"But the most stunning event occurred a couple of months ago," Denise said. "Years ago she had given me a special fluorite crystal pendant and for the past couple of years it had been missing. Turning the house topsy-turvy several times never produced the gem. I was distraught as my mom had had a special purpose in mind when she gave me the gem."

One night Denise's mother visited her in a dream. Denise told her mother she was upset that she couldn't find the pendant and her mother promised to find it. "When I got up the next morning and went into the kitchen for coffee, I spied something on the floor that hadn't been there the night before," Denise said. "It was my fluorite pendant." Denise called out to her boyfriend who was also surprised because he hadn't seen the pendant there earlier.

"There was no other explanation for the sudden appearance of the stone other than Mother really did find the stone for me as promised," Denise said. "I began to cry and said out loud, 'Thanks Mom.' I gazed up at her photo on the wall and I swear she winked at me."

24

Red Eyes in the Darkness

D ry brown leaves cover the floor of deer hunter Chris Black's wooded property near Park Hills in Southeast Missouri. Black keeps a small camper there during deer and turkey seasons and, while he sleeps in the camper to get an early start, motion-controlled digital cameras strapped to trees take photographs of, hopefully, deer.

He captured lights on those cameras in 2006, lights that shouldn't have been on his property miles away from roads. He captured more this year. Black thinks something highly strange is happening on his property. "The same property, right before deer season, and more strange lights," he said. "This time with three deer in the photo and these lights are fire red."

A daytime photograph shows two deer, one grazing and one apparently startled, maybe by the noise from the camera. Behind the deer is a plane of dead leaves and young trees. All normal. Then there's the night picture.

Three deer, one in the foreground, stand looking at the camera, their eyes shining with the flash reflection. But about ten feet off the ground are two red lights set apart like eyes. "They aren't that hard to see," Black said. "Right above the deers' heads, they look like two red eyeballs without a face."

Taillights? No. The trees in the night picture match the trees in the day picture. There's no room for taillights in these images and the lights are much higher than any truck. But Black sees more than just the lights. "There are a number of things in this photo which disturb me," he said. "The first thing is the odd-looking expressions on the deer themselves. They look as if someone just screamed, 'hey.'" All three deer in this picture are looking directly at the camera. "And they all looked at the camera at once," he said. "None of the other

82

Chris Black's trail cam caught this daylight picture of deer on his property near Park Hills. *Photo courtesy of Chris Black*

photos taken during this three-day time frame show all the deer in the background looking in the direction of the camera at the same time."

Black's camera took sixty-five pictures, many of which have multiple deer in a frame. "Usually, there will be one or two with their heads down feeding, and maybe one looking in the general direction of the camera, but never directly into it," he said. "To me it looks like they are all focused on one thing and sort of mesmerized by it."

After Black downloaded the photographs onto his computer, he took a closer look at the red lights – that one frame the only one with the red lights – and didn't like what he found. "When you zoom in on the red light on the left; now this is going to sound off the chart, but I swear when I zoomed in on it, I can see a face in the light," he said. "It's not at all hard to see. Plain as day there is a little face inside the glow. To me it resembles (a) little devil face."

Black and his father stayed in the camper most of the first week of deer season, Black's brother came the fourth day. That night Black's brother slept in a bed against the far edge of the camper next to the canvas wall. The next morning, something was bother-

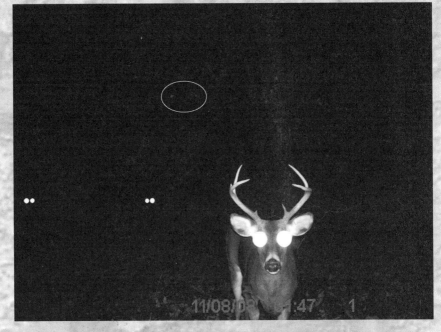

The nighttime picture not only found deer, it captured a pair of glowing red eyes in the night. (Red eyes circled.) *Photo courtesy of Chris Black*

ing Black's brother. During the night, something happened. While Black's brother slept with his arms above his head against the canvas, something touched his arm. "He said he didn't move because he thought it might be a deer's nose pushing against the canvas of the camper," Black said. "He said he wasn't asleep but he felt something solid touching or pushing against the canvas and against his arm. He said it moved from one side of his arm, towards his head, then back along his arm." The brother froze, not wanting to startle whatever was outside. "Then he fell back to sleep," Black said. "It was only then that I told him about capturing the lights on my trail camera. I just think it's awful strange that he would experience something weird like that in the same weekend that I captured more weird (stuff) on my camera."

But Black wouldn't have considered a paranormal explanation for the two red eyes staring at his deer camera if it wasn't for the lights he captured two years before. "It seems like there are just too many things to pass off as imagination, or coincidence," he said. "I'm convinced that this property is haunted. In some way, by something, but I don't know what. But when it gets caught on camera that's hard evidence that I'm not seeing things.

25

Hunting For The Unknown

R yan Straub sees dead people. A car wreck left the then 16-year-old Straub broken, but it may have fixed something in him that had, until that point, lain dormant. "I was hurt really bad," Straub, now 25 and living in Centralia, Missouri, said. "Then I started seeing things, even that night. Spirits. After that I thought, 'What the hell's happening to me?'"

As he saw more and more people – dead people – no one around him could see, he set out to find out what had happened to him. "That's what's sparked my interest in the paranormal," he said. "I've dedicated my life to it. Since then I've been indulging myself in research."

Straub began investigating the paranormal in his hometown of Marceline, Missouri, the boyhood home of Walt Disney, which included a local nursing home, and the "lady in white" that haunts a Marceline restaurant. Straub chose to attend Benedictine University in Lisle, Illinois, because of its paranormal reputation. "It's haunted," he said. "That's the only reason I went to it. It's a Catholic university. There were exorcisms conducted on the top floor of one building. That's why I went to school here. I heard it was haunted by demons."

Today, Straub, along with Jeremy Taylor and Mike Hourcade investigate the paranormal with their group Tir Firnath, which means, "to observe the dead" in Tolkien elvish. They also, if asked, try to rid an area of any unwanted spirits. "The three of us started doing extensive research," Straub said. "I like to call our group an 'evaluate and eradication' group. We'll go into an area and determine what (type of entity) is there and get rid of it. I don't like going somewhere and not help someone."

Straub's group has investigated spots in Idaho, Illinois, Missouri, and Oklahoma, and although the group specializes in hauntings, they'll also entertain reports of aliens, Bigfoot, and werewolves. Tir Firnath has received a report of an Ohio man witnessing what looked like a large dog walking on two legs near a construction site and one report from Missouri. "A friend heard stuff in the woods and he saw what looked like a large wolf-like creature walking around the property," he said. "That's probably the most non spirit-related thing we've dealt with."

Straub's most chilling encounter was at Hillhaven (*detailed in Chapter 39*), a nursing home in Marceline that was in the process of closing its doors.

Another one of Straub's investigations was more personal. An old bridge crosses West Yellow Creek just off Jarboe Road in rural Linn County, Missouri. The gravel road between Brookfield and Marceline used to cross the bridge, built in 1920, until a new bridge went up in 1996 for the estimated 35 vehicles that cross that way each day. But people in the area still talk about the old bridge – and its ghosts. Straub knows the stories well.

"It used to be known as Colemine Road," Straub said. "It's like

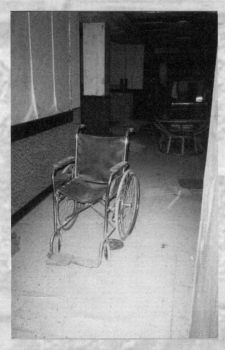

a local legend." According to the legend, a little boy whose family lived on Colemine Road was struck and killed by a truck as he rode his tricycle on the gravel road. On nights of a full moon, people may catch a glimpse of the boy. Another story has a man being killed on the bridge by thieves. "There was a man when it was Colemine Road walking home from a party," Straub said. "He was drinking and was picked up, mugged, and had the crap beat out of him and left to die

A dark figure lurks in the background of a picture taken by paranormal investigator Ryan Straub at the abandoned Hillhaven nursing home in Marceline. *Photo courtesy of Ryan Straub*

by an old bridge. He haunts that bridge down there and he can be pretty vengeful."

Locals say visitors to the old bridge often report feeling like some-one is watching them. Straub first investigated the legends of Jarboe Road at about 1 or 2 a.m., June 13, 2003 – a Friday the 13th – during a full moon. "Those are the stories I went down there to investigate," Straub said. "When I went there I didn't see either one."

But something was there. When Straub stepped from his vehicle, the area felt strange.

"It was extremely quiet," Straub said. "What's weird about that is it was summer; locusts and all sorts of noises you can hear. It was almost too quiet. That uneasy calm feeling." As Straub approached the bridge, he found he wasn't alone. "Where that bridge is, there's not a whole lot around it," he said. "I was by myself. I kept hearing something telling me to come down under the bridge." The voice was male and insistent. "It sounded like a younger man. I was 19. It sounded like he was 25 to 30 maybe," he said. "The average man's voice sounding like he wanted me to come down there."

Who the hell's out here with me? ran through Straub's head, as he felt the hair stand on the back of his neck. "My shock got turned into curiosity," he said. "Which will (one day) most probably get me in trouble." Straub flicked on his flashlight, the beam cutting through the darkness, and crawled down the embankment toward the underside of the bridge. "I'm either stupid or crazy or a little bit of both," he said. "There was nothing down there. There was no one down there. There was no one in the woods. Something was calling for me, but nothing was down there."

After searching under the bridge and the nearby trees, Straub went back to his car, but the road wasn't finished with him. "As I was leaving, I was about halfway down the road and it looked like a dog was running toward the car," he said. "It was a huge black dog. It jumped in front of the car and I hit it, but my car went right through it. That thing got me."

The voice calling him in the night, and the spectral dog piqued Straub's curiosity. He's sure the legends of the road being haunted are true, and that's drawn him back – many times. "I went down there about ten nights in ten years but that's the only thing I ever had happen," he said. "I talked to everyone in the area and they all told me the same story. There's either something that happened, or it's legend."

26

The Beast by the Lake

*T*he early morning of March 21 was warm, about fifty degrees, when the truck pulled into the crescent-shaped driveway at Pleasant Hill Lake. "It was dark, but your eyes had adjusted and you could tell the difference in the shadows of the darkness," Ben said. Ben and Marli were inside that truck, and they wish the night had been darker.

"Saturday night I had to do an upgrade for a client and I had to start at 11 p.m. and wasn't going to finish until about 3," he said. "I said, let's go for a pop and go for a drive." After grabbing a soda, the two drove to the lake under a moonless sky. "We drove out to the Pleasant Hill Lake," Ben said. "On the back side of the lake there's this one place I'd been fishing a lot over the past fifteen, sixteen years. I'd been out there by myself at night catfishing."

Truck tires crunched across gravel as Ben pulled onto the back side of the lake toward a concrete square with a picnic table. People can fish right off the concrete. When Ben put the truck in park, his window was facing the water, Marli's was facing crescent drive. Ben left the truck running so they could listen to the radio, but soon he shut the truck off and they cracked the windows. A slight breeze brought the night through the cab of the truck.

"(Marli) is real easy to freak out," Ben said. "I started talking about what her kids and my kid talked about, which was a Bigfoot." Ben started making monkey noises out the window, trying to scare Marli, but he soon stopped. After talking for about fifteen more minutes, a strange smell crept into the truck. "I was like, what was that weird smell?" Ben said. "I couldn't make out what it was. It wasn't an overpowering smell. It was just enough to smell it."

Marli suggested the smell was from earlier fishermen cleaning their fish on that spot. But something else was odd.

Ben noticed a light from a nearby farmhouse above a tree line about twenty-five feet away started blinking. "The light kind of went away then it came back on," he said. "I thought, no big deal." Then the light went completely out. They soon found this was because something was standing in front of it.

"(Ben) said, 'I feel like we're being watched,'" Marli said. "We were sitting there talking and then that thing came up on that gravel road and I was like, oh my gosh."

As they sat in the cab of the truck, something tall, broad, and bipedal stepped from the trees and onto the gravel road. "As it did that she said, 'something is coming, and I'm not joking,'" Ben said. "I saw it step out."

The figure was black in the moonless night, but the two could make it out from its surroundings. "You could see the outline of it," Ben said. "The minute it stepped out on the road and I saw it, it was the weirdest feeling I've ever had in my life. My mind was telling me something wasn't right but I couldn't pinpoint what it was, but I could not take my eyes off it."

The dark figure walked onto the right side of the gravel road and worked itself to the far left side of the road to give itself a wide berth of Ben's truck.

"We didn't know if it didn't know if we were there," Ben said.

As the thing approached, in what Ben and Marli said was a strong, confident stride, Ben's bad feeling got worse. "I think it's because I couldn't rationalize what it was," Ben said.

The thing's broad shoulders swung as it walked, although Ben and Marli only occasionally saw its arms swinging in the darkness. They couldn't make out its hands. But what confused the two was its head. "Marli said it kind of looked like someone wearing a hooded sweatshirt because of the head," Ben said. "The head came up, but to me the head didn't look as tall as a normal human being's head. As the shoulder came up it transitioned right into the head."

Because of the darkness, neither Ben nor Marli could make out facial features, but they both agree it wasn't human. "When I realized this really wasn't a person with a hooded sweatshirt, you could tell where the hair came to a point. It didn't look like a hood," Marli said. "It looked like hair."

The thing walked within twenty feet from the truck and neither Ben nor Marli could hear it in the gravel. "You could have heard a pin drop. There was no crunching of any gravel," Marli said. "The window was cracked and I didn't notice any breathing, but I was so petrified. It was so bizarre. I've never felt like that and I don't ever want to feel like that again."

As the creature came closer, Ben noticed it seemed to be leaning forward as it walked. "It walked right past us," Ben said. "As it was walking up it had this really strange stride. Not really hunched over. It had a real strong powerful stride to it." As it stepped even with the cab of the truck, the two froze in fear. "The shoulders got real broad," Ben said. "And the whole upper body actually turned. I knew whatever it was stared right at me as it walked by." Ben gauges the creature's height somewhere between 6'2" and 6'5".

"It walked by and as it got to the other road it stopped," he said. "There's like a hill that runs down the road and it was standing next to the hill. She couldn't see it. I could only see part of it." As Ben stared at the thing, only seeing its head and shoulders against the hill, he knew they had to go. "At that point, there was no question. We were leaving," he said. "As I started the truck and I hit my break lights that head went up the hill and was gone."

Ben and Marli are convinced they saw Bigfoot that night and it's changed their lives. "I didn't believe in it," Ben said. "I thought it was made up stuff. I don't know if I'll ever be the same. When I go out at night now I always have the lights on in front of the house and go right for my truck. I don't want to see it again."

Marli's house is at the edge of Pleasant Hill, a tree line and fields sit across the road from her property. "I've never been afraid of the dark, but I won't even go outside after dark now. I just won't," she said. "I make sure the blinds are completely shut. I was completely freaked out. I never believed in (Bigfoot). I thought it was a hoax. Then after we saw what we saw I got on the Internet and started reading it. These people were saying the same exact thing I just saw. I don't know if I'll ever be the same after this. Even thinking about it sends chills up my spine."

Marli won't stay in her house alone after dark and disturbing dreams about Bigfoot trouble her nights. The encounter has her second-guessing what she allows her children to do. "I haven't talked with them about it," she said. "I don't like them going out after dark now. I don't like it at all. I can't keep them from doing it because they'll go, what's up? But as far as going across the street in those fields and the woods, I won't let them go."

Ben and Marli were so troubled by their encounter, they contacted Bigfoot researcher Randy Harrington of Leavenworth, Kansas. "They seem believable," Harrington said. "We're going to go up and check out the area. All we can do is go through the area and look for the signs. As far as their story, it's as believable as anyone's story I've heard or interviewed." The silence of the creature as it walked past Ben and Marli is common, Harrington said. "You and I are used to hearing people walk across gravel with hard-soled shoes," Harrington said. "If they weren't wearing shoes you might not hear anything. How can it remain so hidden from so many smart people? They've got to be silent."

The area around Pleasant Hill has had its number of Bigfoot reports over the years. "It's a good area," Harrington said. "You've got some decent wooded areas there that would possibly harbor a small population of that creature."

Although both Ben and Marli said they would never go back to that spot, on March 26 they did. "When we went back out there and saw where it took place I feel better about it," Marli said. "Although it rained that Monday, you can definitely tell someone was walking. There were broken branches. There was the first part of the footprints. You could tell there were three toes in the front. On one of the trees the bark had been peeled away and was laying right there. I'll never say I don't believe in anything again."

27

Is There a Buried City Beneath Moberly, Missouri?

*T*he newspaper story was sensational – in all sense of the word. The tale is incredible and written in the era when journalism meant whatever sold papers, truth be damned. But the story is about an underground city and giants in the Midwest, so it's worth telling again.

It happened on the pages of the April 9, 1885, edition of *The New York Times* in a story entitled: "Missouri's buried city: A strange discovery in a coal mine near Moberly." Moberly, the largest city in Randolph County, had a population of 6,108 in the 1880s.

Coal miners, sinking a shaft 360 feet deep, broke into a cavern revealing "a wonderful buried city," the article claimed. Lava arches stretched across the roof of the cavern, looming over the streets of an ancient city "which are regularly laid out and enclosed by walls of stone, which is cut and dressed in a fairly good, although rude style of masonry."

Workers, along with Moberly city recorder David Coates and Moberly city marshal George Keating, inspected the site, found a 30-by-100-feet hall in the cavern filled with stone benches and hand tools. "Further search disclosed statues and images made of a composition closely resembling bronze, lacking luster," the article read.

Explorers discovered a stone fountain in a wide court, still pouring "perfectly pure water" into its basin. But it was what lay beside the fountain that interested the people exploring the site. "Lying beside the foundation (of the fountain) were portions of the skeleton of a human being," according to the article. "The bones of the leg measured, the femur four and one-half feet, the tibia four feet and three inches, showing that when alive the figure was three times the size of an ordinary man, and possessed of a wonderful muscular power and quickness."

Its skull, the story reported, was shattered; bronze tools, granite hammers, metallic saws and flint knives were scattered all around. "They are not so highly polished, nor so accurately made as those now finished by our best mechanics, but they show skill and an evidence of an advanced civilization that are very wonderful," according to the article.

Explorers spent twelve hours in the buried city and resurfaced only after the oil in their lamps burned low. "No end to the wonders of the discovery was reached," the article stated. "A further extended search will be made in a day or two." No record of the extended search could be found.

Dr. Tom Spencer, a professor in the department of History, Humanities, Philosophy and Political Science at Northwest Missouri State University, said that's because after printing the story, the newspapers tried to forget it. "A lot of the time I think these stories were written based entirely off hearsay and little or no direct on-site reporting," he said. "As the story grew, the details got more and more outrageous."

He equates it to a childhood game where children sit in a circle and one child whispers a story into another's ear and by the time the story completes the circle, it was completely different. "The point of this exercise was to try to see what would happen when the story had made it all the way around the circle," he said. "If you recall, sometimes the 'finished story' bore little resemblance to the original story. My guess is one element of this story is factual – like the strange shaft formation or a long femur was found – and it became more and more embellished as it went around the journalistic circle at the time."

So what happened to the fabulous buried city under Moberly, Missouri? "There were stories like this periodically at the time and they usually disappear quietly because someone goes to investigate and there's nothing to it," Spencer said. "In order to avoid the embarrassment the newspapers just don't say anything else about it."

28

The Ghosts of
Central Methodist University

C entral Methodist University has anchored the small town of Fayette, Missouri, since its doors opened in September 1857. During the past 150-plus years, a number of people have died at the university – and some may still there, awaiting graduation.

Ghostly stories, of knocks, taps, footsteps and apparitions are associated with dormitories. "Howard-Payne is where all the whacky stuff happens," said Melanie Morrison, a former financial assistance counselor at the university.

A stone outside the Howard-Payne dormitory reads "Howard Female College." While the college refurbished the dormitory in the 1940s, a falling brick killed a student, reported the campus newspaper, *The Talon*. Since then, her spirit has appeared outside the dorm, but more typically is experienced inside the building, turning electrical appliances on and off, knocking on doors and rattling pipes.

But bigger things happen at the conservatory.

Sean Maples' supernatural investigation group Missouri Paranormal visited the university and is convinced something haunts the building. "We spend most of our time debunking things and I would say ninety percent of the stuff we run across we can explain," he said. "But it was one of most interesting ones that we've done. We really had a lot of weird experiences." The building moaned. "It was probably right around one in the morning. It was just me and one other investigator in the whole building," he said. "We were probably two feet apart. It was so loud I was surprised the

The ghost of band director Tom Birch has been seen outside Swinney Conservatory of Music since he died there May 1, 1964, while conducting the piece "The Catacombs" at the annual spring concert.

The Conservatory has graced the campus of Central Methodist University for eight decades.

other team members outside the building didn't hear it. It literally echoed through this church."

The noise died as quickly as it filled the sanctuary and, Maples realized, it came from the side of the building that held the exits. "We decided to go downstairs in complete darkness and out of the auditorium in complete darkness to get out of that building," he said. "It spooked me a little bit. We went back in there and could not determine the cause of it." The heat was not on in the building, nor was the air conditioning. Maples' group has been back twice and has not been able to explain the noise by natural means.

In the auditorium, Maples and other investigators have heard voices "like whispers." Maples has captured a number of these on audio in the form of Electronic Voice Phenomenon or EVP (voices recorded in an empty room). "One of the weirdest things we caught on EVP was a cat," Maples said. "There's a cat meowing in the basement of the church. We looked all over and couldn't find it. We really didn't find that significant at all, until the second visit we captured an EVP of a man in the auditorium talking about a cat."

That man may be former band director Tom Birch, who died in that room May 1, 1964, while conducting the piece, "The Catacombs," from Mussorgsky's "Pictures at an Exhibition" at the annual spring concert. Jim Steele, owner and publisher of *The Fayette Advertiser* and *The Democrat-Leader*, was a senior at the university and was in the auditorium when Birch had a heart attack. "It was kind of a warm pleasant spring evening," Steele said. "He had the white starched shirt, tails. Just as he had gotten into (The Catacombs) there was a 'whoo,' a gasp you could hear in the audience." Birch dropped onto the stage, fell into the drum set and died.

Since then, people occasionally report seeing a man in a tuxedo who looks like Dr. Birch standing in front of the auditorium smoking a cigar – such as the image a student saw in the 1970s. "A girl was going from the student union across campus to Cross Memorial Clock Tower on the campus' quadrangle," said Robert Bray, Central's Alumni Director at the time. "The apparition appeared and said, 'Nice evening for a concert.'" Frightened, the girl convinced her boyfriend to go with her to the conservatory. She found a picture of the man she'd seen – it was Dr. Birch. "You can tell it's a male in the church, the voices we captured," Maples said.

Other spirits that reportedly haunt Central Methodist University are N. Louise Wright, dean of the conservatory of music, who died much like Birch, during a performance, and the ghost of a young stable boy who was killed on the university grounds during the Civil War. During the group's last visit to the university, they captured an EVP that may have been the stable boy asking for help. "Each one of us carried a two-way radio; they're all on the same channel," he said. "When (the child's voice) happened, two of the people with radios were standing next to me and mine was the only one that went off – it was a kid."

Missouri Paranormal approaches reported hauntings as skeptics, treating orbs and bumps in the night first as things that can be explained terrestrially. But they couldn't explain the Central Methodist University hauntings. "A lot of activity we captured didn't really follow the normal expectations of a normal haunting," he said. "It seemed like the activity was very sporadic. It was a hit-or-miss deal. If you weren't in the right spot you didn't experience it."

29

Fishing With Grandpa, One Last Time

B ennett Spring in South Central Missouri pours 100 million gallons of fresh water into the tree-lined Spring Branch each day on its way to the nearby Niangua River. Spring Branch is stocked with rainbow trout for the thousands of fly fishermen who visit the spring each year. "It is absolutely breathtaking," said hunter and fisherman Chris Black, of Park Hills, Missouri. "The water comes straight out of the ground, boils up from the unknown depths below, and fills this magnificent spring full of water."

But in 1998, something other than fishermen visited Bennett Spring – something otherworldly Black wants to believe is true.

Black fishes at the spring a couple of times a summer, picking a three-day weekend and makes a holiday out of it. "This one particular weekend was no different than the rest," he said. "I called and made my reservations like I normally do, got to my room, dumped all my junk, and went fishing."

At the spring, Black put on his waders and stood in front of one of his favorite fishing holes. After a while, he realized he wasn't alone. "While standing there, fishing but not catching, an elderly man walks up beside me," Black said. "I really didn't think that much about it at the time because I rarely look around. I'm so focused on catching fish, that I don't care who's around me; I just do my own thing." But as the man stood next to him in complete silence, Black grew curious. "As I fished, I kept looking a little further to my right and finally got a glimpse of the old guy next to me," he said. "My knees buckled, and I almost went down in the water."

The man standing next to Black was his grandfather, or at least looked like his grandfather – his late grandfather. "He was the exact spitting image," Black said. "I could not believe what I was seeing."

"Are you okay?" the old man asked.

"I stammered for a moment, I guess with my jaw wide open," Black said. "I murmured a 'yes, I'm fine.' Then we began to talk."

Black asked the man about his family, where he was from, and what he had done in his life, but the old man didn't answer – he just gave Black his name. "I came up with nothing," Black said. "The strange thing about this whole incident was that he said that his name was Walter Black." Black's late grandfather's name was Walter Black. "That really threw me," he said. "I went through the whole family routine, and he didn't know anyone in the family." Eventually, the old man just walked away, leaving Black to stand in the stream alone.

"At the start of this, I (felt) that it was a beautiful day, and what a day that I would love to spend with my grandpa," Black said. "I guess maybe I had." Black walked back to his truck, silent tears washing his cheeks. "I had to go sit in my truck for a minute and contemplate what the hell had just happened," he said. "Had he visited me? I would like to think so."

30

Mac Tonnies Makes a Case for Cryptoterrestrials

Betty and Barney Hill were driving from Montreal to New Hampshire on September 19, 1961, when they claim they were taken aboard a UFO. After medical exams and verbal interaction, the Hill's were returned to their car. If their story is true, did space aliens abduct the Hills in one of the most famous UFO cases? Maybe not.

Kansas City writer Mac Tonnies isn't convinced contact with a UFO has anything to do with extraterrestrials. Tonnies, author of "After the Martian Apocalypse," said if UFOs and their crews exist, they may have come from right here on Earth. Tonnies calls them cryptoterrestrials; and he's writing a book about them. "It's not so much a theory as a hypothesis. It's a paradigm I suppose," Tonnies said. "It's basically asking, why not?"

The government, scientists, and Edward J. Ruppelt – head of the 1950s Air Force project investigating flying saucers – have all said most UFO cases are pedestrian. Most. Not all. "In the conventional wisdom (UFOs) are explainable through atmospheric effects or psychology," Tonnies said. "If the real ones exist, it's alien spacecraft coming from another star system. I think we're jumping the gun on that. The evidence doesn't support it."

For evidence, Tonnies looks at the descriptions of UFO occupants, folklore, and the evolution of UFO technology. "We have these beings with larger than normal slanted eyes, small noses, and mouths," he said. "They typically lack hair … and have long fingers – weirdly enough – and long arms. And behavior is often descried in a way that they might be nocturnal. "I wonder if this is a species that lives underground. Not that they evolved underground. If they're real, they're obviously an offshoot of people who went down an evolutionary fork in the road."

All cultures have their stories of little people and usually these creatures – elves, fairies, trolls, and dwarves – live underground. But maybe these stories are more than myth. Scientists found the remains of miniature humans (dubbed Hobbits) in a cave on Flores Island near Indonesia in 2004. The islanders have legends of little people who ate the islander's food and stole their children. Tribesmen eventually exterminated them. "Humans lived side-by-side among a diminutive race and we have proof," Tonnies said, although he has testimony of his own. "I actually spoke to a witness who had a face-to-face encounter with small humanoids in Oregon. They said some interesting things, very cryptic. They were very human looking, but small."

Tonnies also questions the apparently superior technology of UFOs. From the airships of the 1800s to the physics-defying craft of today, UFO technology keeps just out of our reach. "It's kind of one step ahead of us no matter where we are," Tonnies said. "With me it suggests subterfuge. Maybe they're trying to throw us off the scent because we can't go to the stars yet."

If this race of cryptoterrestrials exists – which Tonnies doesn't make claim – they're pretty shy. "They don't want to make contact," he said. "My personal impression is ... they are trying to influence our mythology to benefit them or to at least prolong their civilization. Obviously they're not comfortable with contact."

Tonnies cites the well-publicized Washington, D.C., flyovers of UFOs in 1952 and the 1980 Rendlesham Forest incident in England where multiple RAF personnel reported a UFO near a nuclear facility as proof there is something out there. "(The evidence) points to a nonhuman intelligence, but not extraterrestrial," Tonnies said. "It points to a nonhuman intelligence feigning to an extraterrestrial intelligence. I'm not claiming this is the way it is, (but) it's a viable hypothesis."

31

Old Spirits Are Physical at The Elms

*F*ishing River snakes its way past the Elms Resort Hotel and Spa in Excelsior Springs on its long, tree-lined journey to the Missouri River. Water – but not water from the depths of any river – drew people from across the world to the resort in the early part of the 20th century. The purported healing pow-

Presidents, gangsters, and boxers have stayed at The Elms Resort Hotel in Excelsior Springs – some people who've stayed there have never left.

ers of the town's mineral springs attracted politicians, gangsters, and professional boxers. President Harry S. Truman stayed at The Elms on election night 1948. Hours later he hoisted a copy of the *Chicago Tribune* that boasted "Dewey Defeats Truman" that has since become an iconic photograph.

An Elms Hotel has stood on the grounds since 1888. Hotels there burned down in 1898 and 1910, but the hotel that burned on October 30, 1910 left its mark on the grounds forever. An antique boiler lid, once part of a system that used steam to heat the hotel, is on display downstairs. It survived the fire that rushed through the building during a masquerade ball in 1910, as did the guests who rushed out into the night. However, the scream-ing partygoers left something behind. "They said there were no fatalities," said John Mormino, former front office manager at the Elms from its last restoration in 1998 until 2004. "They didn't take into consideration the coal shovelers." The sound of those coal shovelers striking pipes that run through the walls once rang out on the ground floor of the hotel almost every night. "You can hear them banging on pipes still in the walls," Mormino said in 2004. "But the pipes are not hooked up to the heating system." Further work has removed the pipes altogether, said Keith Winge, director of sales and marketing for The Elms.

Other ghostly visitations at The Elms include the hum of a phantom vacuum sweeper, the spirit of a bootlegger that haunts the hotel's European lap pool, a little girl who walks the third floor and disappears through a wall, and the ghost of a maid wearing a 1920s-style uniform. Members of the housekeeping staff who've seen her have said she looks like she's supervising them. And, of course, Elvis.

"People have seen a ghost that looks like Elvis Presley," Winge said – although no one claims the ghost is actually Elvis. "In the 1970s, there used to be an Elvis impersonator that used to per-form here. He is supposed to have committed suicide by jumping out the window." People – guests and staff alike – have reported seeing The Man in White, an apparition in a white jumpsuit with sequins, in the downstairs theater that was a dance club in the 1970s, Winge said. The Man in White disappears into a wall where a staircase used to be – the spot where the Elvis impersonator made his entrance and exit into the club.

But some of the spirits of The Elms are more subtle. In 2006, a couple staying in room 438 got a fright when they looked at a picture the husband took of his wife in their room. Behind the

An antique boiler lid, once part of the Elms heating system, survived the fire that rushed through the building during a masquerade ball in 1910 – the coal shovelers weren't so lucky.

wife was a pasty white human face, with large black eyes and a demure expression, staring from the television. "She was sitting on the bed when her husband took a picture," Winge said. "The TV was off."

Guests have reported feeling someone sitting on the end of their bed and a human hand resting on their shoulder, although there was no other person in the room at the time. "A woman claimed something held her down on the bed for several hours," Winge said. "Which was interesting to file with our insurance company."

But ghosts aren't confined to the hotel. Guests and employees have seen activity on the grounds; an angry man in a white T-shirt and pants paces the gazebo.

Paranormal investigator Sean Maples and his research group, Missouri Paranormal, visited The Elms in April 2009 to discover any truth in the stories. "We just felt like with the history of the building, the likelihood of having a haunting being legit there would probably be pretty high," Maples said.

Part of that history involves gangster Al Capone, who visited The Elms so much during Prohibition, he had his own room. That's where Missouri Paranormal began its investigation. "A

The ghost of a bootlegger has been seen floating face-down in the Elms European lap pool.

meeting room above the front desk, at one point, it was Capone's gambling room," Maples said. "We got an EVP of a woman." Maples asked in the quiet room if anyone else there had something to say. Missouri Paranormal's audio recorders captured a female voice saying, "Yes. I do." Maples said the voice is important because there were no women in the room. But Capone's room wasn't the hotbed of paranormal occurrences in the hotel.

"At The Elms, they have a lot of reports of activity," Maples said. "(Most of) the activity that we captured was all downstairs in the basement."

The lower floor of The Elms is home to a European lap pool, saunas, exercise room, and something much less relaxing. People have reported seeing the body of a bootlegger floating face down in the lap pool. The air was humid and thick when Maples' group ventured downstairs and walked into the lap pool room. Although Maples' group didn't see the bootlegger, they did see something they can't explain. "Three different of our investigators witnessed shadows move in the hallway," Maples said. "The (shadows) would black out the doorway when going by. At first we were concerned we were just matrixing (optical illusions caused when immersed in darkness), but the third time someone said this, we took it seriously."

Outside the lap pool room, where the walking shadows blocked light from the hallway, is the weight room. A Missouri Paranormal investigator stationed himself in the weight room to collect EVPs at about 1:30 a.m. – and wasn't disappointed. "He said (into the empty room), 'I'm going to go now. This is the end of the EVP session,'" Maples said. "In the background you hear a female voice saying, 'Don't go.'" The EVP brought the rest of the group into the room, but it was the only voice they captured there. Something, however, caught them.

"The biggest experience of the whole night unfortunately happened to me," Maples said.

The group tried out a newly purchased meter that monitors static electricity. They placed the meter in the center of the weight room and backed ten feet away – then the fun began. "(We) were getting really great responses," Maples said. "We could get this entity or whatever it was down there to light it up on command. We'd tell it, 'if you walk toward the meter it will light up.' It went on for five or ten minutes; then it just kind of stopped." So Maples pushed it.

"I had this brainstorm that if I taunt it a little bit, just maybe I'd get it to come back out," he said. "A lot of times we'll play good cop/bad cop. 'Are you lonely down here? How long have you been down here?' Another investigator said, 'I don't think there's anything here and if so, it's too much of a coward to come out,' that sort of thing." As Maples taunted the entity, pain suddenly lanced through the back of his neck. "I thought, 'great, I got bit by a spider,'" he said. "I told my wife, 'I just got bit, you need to check this.' She came around and looked at my back and said, 'that's not a bite mark.'" Under Maples shirt she found a six to eight-inch long white scratch mark welted about one-eighth inch.

"I got to admit, it shook me up a little bit," he said. "Over the past eight years I've had experiences of being touched, or something tugging your shirt, but nothing that brought pain on." The mark was barely visible by morning, but that night it disturbed Maples enough, he left the investigation for about an hour. Although he's taunted entities to get a reaction before, nothing's ever left a mark. "Personally I think maybe she, or he, or whoever did it, was just giving me a little bit of a warning," he said. "Maybe I was just pushing my luck."

One legend about The Elms some staff members will swear by is the chandeliers in the banquet hall – they swing. Marbles said it's for no ghostly reason. "The only thing that we were really disappointed in, we got a lot of stories from the staff about how the chandeliers in the banquet hall move," he said. "It took us about two hours to debunk that. They swing, but by natural causes." After playing with the heating system, investigators discovered the chandeliers only moved when the fans kicked on.

The EVPs, the flashing meter and the walking shadows all showed the members of Missouri Paranormal that something haunts The Elms. The scratch, however, proved it to them. "Interaction always seems spooky because they acknowledge your presence," Maples said. "It makes you wonder how many times something's in the room watching you. It's really kind of unnerving."

Although The Elms management once avoided the topic of ghosts, today's management doesn't shy away from the fact that something rarely seen may inhabit this historic hotel. It's even mildly promoted on The Elms website. "We have (embraced it)," Winge said. "We've had a great response. It's brought us more guests than it has deterred."

32

A Haunting in St. Charles

As twelve-year-old Chris Wham and his family watched construction workers build their home in a St. Charles, Missouri, subdivision; everything looked fine. It was 1979. By 1980, Wham wasn't so sure. "In the summer of 1979, my family moved into its first new house," Wham said. "Not just a new house to us, but a brand new house. In the months before the house was completed, my step-father would drive us out to it and we would watch the men work on it."

The land was once an apple orchard and sat almost empty as the house went up. "Our house was one of the first few completed on the street," Wham said. "So I spent much of the year watching the other houses getting built and making new friends whenever kids would move in."

A year went by and Wham's family had comfortably settled in the house. "It was towards end of summer 1980, school had just started the week before, and I was already playing hooky," he said. "I just didn't want to go to school that day, so I faked a stomach ache so I could stay home." Wham stayed in his room until his mother had to go on an errand. "Near twelve noon, my mother asked me to keep an eye on my baby brother while she ran to the store for more diapers," he said.

The round trip to the store, Wham figured, might take fifteen minutes, and his little brother was sleeping, so he had time to play. "I told her I would. I'd do anything to get her out of the house, so I could turn off her horrible soap operas," he said. "As soon as she left, I hopped into the big brown La-Z-Boy recliner that was parked in front of the TV and changed over to Channel 11. It was now exactly noon and *Green Acres* was just coming on."

As he sat there, the sound of the program drifting through the living room, Wham knew he wasn't alone. "No sooner had the theme song ended did I hear, and feel, a rapping over my left shoulder on the back of the big La-Z-Boy," he said. "A soft thumpity thump, thumpity thump, thumpity thump. The same type of sound an impatient person might create with his fingers on a desk." Wham was sure his mother had come home and he was in trouble.

"My first and immediate thought was … 'Wow, she's back quick. She must be checking up on me. How did she get in so quietly?'" he said. But a car hadn't pulled up to the house. No car door creaked open, nor did one close. No footsteps came up the stairs. Fear clutched Wham's stomach. "As the thumping continued, I turned my head up and to the left, expecting to see my mother hovering over me," Wham said.

Something was hovering over him, but it wasn't his mother. "I saw a ghostly hand and arm tapping its fingers on the back of my chair," Wham said. "From the position I was in, I couldn't see much farther than the elbow, nor did I want to look any farther." The entity appeared to be grayish-white and translucent, like smoke – except for the arm. "The outline of the hand and arm was very well defined," he said. "I could clearly see the veins and tendons on the back of the hand. The fingers were long and thin with long pointy, dirty fingernails. On the middle finger was a large ring, that even through the transparency of the apparition, appeared to be silver with a large oval black stone in the center."

Wham turned back toward the television, hoping the arm would go away – it didn't. The thumpity thump went on. "I tried to act like I didn't just see anything," he said. "I tried to block it from my mind. Then, from across the house, I heard my baby brother as he began to cry." The crying broke Wham's fear. He launched himself out of the chair and ran to his brother's room holding him until their mother returned. "As soon as she arrived, I told her my story and she didn't believe me," Wham said. "By this time in my life, I had gained a reputation for being a practical joker, and my mother thought this was just another one of my tricks. It most certainly was not."

Many years have now past at the home without incident, but something lingers in Wham's mind. "I do not know if this has anything to do with this story, but the very next day after I saw the hand, I returned from school to find our yard had been tilled over and grass seed had been planted," he said. "As I walked up and down the rows, freshly dug into the yard, I found my first arrowhead. I've long since lost it, but I've always wondered if it had something to do with the ghostly hand."

33

Windyville
and The Internet Curse

A woman with the head of a goat. A spectral hitchhiker. Red eyes that stare at passersby from the dead, black windows of abandoned buildings. This is the legend of Windyville, Missouri. "Visitors have reported screams from the old cannery building, and a horseback rider was spotted at Lone Rock Cemetery. It's also home to spiritual cults, so watch out," proclaimed an October 20, 2005 article in *USA Today*.

Sounds like a great place to hunt ghosts, right? Not really.

Ronnie Powell lives in Windyville, a town many sites on the Internet say is a ghost town. It's not. The town was once home to a tomato cannery, grocery store, post office and a number of families. The buildings are still there, but the businesses aren't, and only four or five houses are occupied. "Windyville looks deserted," Powell said. "But real live people live here." The population of Windyville grows, however, when ghost hunters are in town. "(These) people came to Windyville and they pilfered, they broke into buildings, they had rituals, and it got so bad that we got the law to get rid of most of them," he said. "They told them not to come back."

Powell, who retired after thirty years with the Missouri Department of Conservation, has always liked to write and once penned a few Windyville ghost stories for *More Missouri Ghosts*, by Joan Gilbert. He wrote the stories as fiction but they were published as fact. Although the stories were left out of the next edition of the book, they'd already hit the Internet. "I know (the trouble) is all because of me and my stories," he said. "'The Ghosts of Windyville' was just tidbits of things that I couldn't corroborate. They were just stories. I sure did ruin Windyville."

Ghost hunters and the curious have vandalized the buildings, trespassed and terrorized the few residents of the town. "The stories I could write about the ghost hunters would be better than the ghost stories," Powell said. "They wouldn't want people looking in their windows."

Although people have trespassed around his home, nothing bothered him as badly as the Goths. "They had some kind of a fire ritual down here," he said. "I ran them off. They all ganged up around me. I told them I was armed and they scattered. They were dancing around a fire and were chanting and all that. One man had a knife. I saw that."

The School of Metaphysics in Windyville probably hasn't helped the town's reputation. "They picked Windyville as the ninth (most haunted) place," Dr. Barbara Condron of the School of Metaphysics said of the *USA Today* article. "They picked dead places. Windyville isn't dead." The school, which has fifteen branches throughout the Midwest, focuses on channeling the mind's energy in positive ways and learning how to co-exist with your fellow man – but the locals don't always view it that way. "We're kind of the talk of the high school here," Condron said. "A lot of times we get joke calls. 'Ah, yes, you guys move things with your mind out there?' It's the Uri Geller bending spoons thing. It hasn't been good."

And the school has experienced trespassing and vandalism, too; much like a recent incident. "Two guys who graduated Lebanon High School were going to chain our gate to their pickup, tear it down and drag it down the road," Condron said. "They were fortunately caught by local authorities."

The nature of the School of Metaphysics calls for thinking positively. The school rarely prosecutes – it didn't in this case – and Condron said she doesn't think the kids from Lebanon will come back. "It's one thing to do it in the night time and another to look the people in the eye the next day," she said. "It's the golden rule in Christianity. You treat people the way you want to be treated. I hope it heals."

Today, the Windyville ghost stories remain on dozens of ghost hunter websites, which means Windyville may not be off the paranormal map anytime soon. "It's Pandora's box. It's already been opened," Condron said. "Technology brings good to the world, but there's always a dark side."

34

Gravity Hill

On a quiet country road west of Freeman, Missouri, past railroad tracks and between two hills, almost throwing distance from the Kansas state line, sits a flat spot in the gravel. Some locals, like Kylie Guier of Freeman, claim that if you stop on that spot and put your vehicle in neutral, the car will start moving, sometimes up to twenty-five miles per hour.

People say gravity doesn't work there.

"Everybody calls it Gravity Hill," Guier said. "It's out on this gravel road in the middle of nowhere. I don't know anyone who's an expert on it. Everyone just knows it's there." Guier's been to Gravity Hill a number of times, as have most area people she knows, and, "I've never known anybody it hasn't worked for."

It didn't work for Jake Koehn of nearby Adrian, Missouri. "(My friends and I) went there around 6 p.m. during the summer, so plenty of daylight," he said. "We parked at the bottom of the hill, put the truck in neutral and did not see much for a result. After about ten minutes, we gave up on it and left." He may have given up too soon.

Urban legend has it if you sprinkle flour or gravel dust on the trunk of the car, drivers will later find child-sized handprints in the dust. I'm so there.

I pulled my minivan onto 299th Street (much too gravelly and rural to be called a street) from Route D in Cass County on a clear September afternoon. Sure I was in a minivan, not the Mystery Machine, but I think a minivan's what the Scooby gang drove when they grew up.

The lane leading to Gravity Hill is surrounded by wavy pasture-land, the occasional pond and patches of sunflowers breaking the swaths of green. Over the railroad tracks and up two hills – according

On a spot between these hills near Freeman, cars are said to move by themselves.

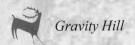

I wanted to find a flat spot to test Gravity Hill. I found one.

to many listings on the Internet – you're supposed to drive to the end of the lane, turn around and come to rest at the bottom. Then the magic happens.

Many people who've been to Gravity Hill claim the moving car phenomenon is an optical illusion and, as I parked the minivan at a spot between hills that looked flat, I found it wasn't. The level I brought to Gravity Hill showed where I'd parked was anything but level. So, when I put the vehicle in neutral, it moved.

Duh.

I let the minivan coast farther down the hill and checked the road again. Not level. But the next time I stopped, I found a spot in the road that was flat. I moved the level all around my vehicle and the ground was sufficiently flat enough the minivan shouldn't move unless it became so embarrassed from being a minivan it collapsed.

Okay. The ground was flat. I marked the spot, hopped into the driver's seat and slid the gear into neutral. The minivan moved immediately. Three mph, five mph, seven mph, the sound of gravel popping beneath the tires carried through the open windows of the minivan's cab. The van stopped halfway up the hill and I put my foot on the brake to keep it from rolling back down.

Sweet.

I took my foot off the brake and, yes, the van rolled back down. After I placed the minivan back onto the flat spot, I ran the level around the van again. Yep. Still flat. I did this six more times. Five times my vehicle seemed to move of its own volition. One time it just sat there and a bee flew through the cab.

On one of my seven runs, the mini-van got up to eleven mph.

The mini-van tried to escape.

Driving away from Gravity Hill, not one darned fingerprint on my bumper, I realized I'd been a part of something weird. Could Gravity Hill be an optical illusion? Sure. Even after I'd determined the ground was flat and my van shouldn't have moved, I'm willing to consider that. It's still a mystery.

35

Approached by Black-Eyed Kids

*T*he children looked out of place in the night. Missourian Craig Besand walked down the street toward his flat in Norwich, England, when two figures approached him. "They appeared to be young boys," Besand said. "One was about thirteen years old, the other one was about nine."

At the time, Besand was studying abroad at the University of East Anglia in Norwich. "I('d been) at a friend's house having a few drinks until the late hours," he said. "My friend asked me if I was all right to walk back to my flat and if I wanted I could crash on his couch. I told him I would be all right, I just wanted to get home and go to bed. It was after one in the morning." Between Besand's flat and his friend's flat was a cemetery – that's where he saw the children.

"My friend lives up the street from a very old cemetery on Dereham Road," Besand said. "I walk past this cemetery every time I go to his house." He'd made it a few blocks when he saw two figures approach him. "They were both wearing hoodies, sneakers; typical kid stuff," Besand said. "The older one said that they were trying to find the graveyard and that they were lost." The older one asked Besand, "could you please take us there?"

The age of the children and the late night struck Besand as strange. "I figured it was odd that young kids were hanging out in graveyards at this time of night," he said. "But kids are into whatever so I agreed to take them there. They asked me very politely and the cemetery was on my way home anyway." As Besand escorted the boys toward the cemetery, he looked at them closer. The oldest boy's hair was black, "his skin was porcelain white and veiny." Then Besand saw the eyes. "They both had eyes that were as dark as coal, no sign of white," Besand said. "The eyes were the most distinct features, it was like they had no souls or nothing inside of them."

116

He asked these Black-Eyed Children where they lived. They named a nearby street. "I thought that was strange because this cemetery is huge and almost everyone in town knows where it is," he said. When they reached the cemetery gates, the older one asked Besand to come in with them.

"I told them no, I was going home," he said. "He asked me again to go in with them. I still told him no." The younger Black-Eyed Child, Besand noticed, appeared nervous. "(He had) this look of anxiety about him," Besand said. "Then the older one stopped *asking* me. He started to make a demand for me to go into the graveyard with them." Then the older child's demeanor changed. "The frustration on this kid's face was trying to be hidden behind one of the most evil grins that I ever saw," Besand said. "My heart was pounding in my throat at this time as the older one said, 'we wouldn't harm you,' with that grin on his face."

The grin, Besand found, was hypnotic. "Oddly enough, I was becoming more drawn to him and I was thinking that I should go in with them," he said. "Then the silent younger kid said something that scared the hell out of me. The younger one said, 'We shouldn't be doing this.' Immediately after he spoke, I snapped out of my trance," Besand said. "My flight-or-fight instinct kicked in and I ran as fast as I could. I looked back to see if they were running after me, but they had vanished. I ran all the way home."

About a week later, Besand wandered into a magic shop whose owner, he discovered, was Wiccan. "I bought some incense and then got into a conversation about me being an American, traveling, and then about haunted places in town," he said. "So I told her my story of the Black-Eyed Children. She told me that I wasn't imagining anything."

Besand asked her what they were. "She told me that no one knows," he said. "The people who found that out aren't here to tell about it. She said they could have been anything from demons to fairies." He asked her why they would want him to go willingly with them to the cemetery. "She said that they could just want something from you or they could have taken me to their realm," he said. "She also told me that I did the right thing by running away, and that I'm never going to find out what they were so I'm better off just going on with my life and not thinking too much about it. I tell other people about it and they either get creeped out or they have a good laugh at my expense."

36

Night of the Dogman

*T*he silent cemetery in Chariton County, Missouri, hides at the end of a slice of gravel snaking into hills. A dark roof of trees turns the long stretch of rocks and dirt into a leafy tunnel leading into a graveyard. The most notable resident there is Pettis Perkinson, a pre-Civil War farmer whose slave, B.K. Bruce, would later become the first black Treasurer of the United States. The locals call the area Hojo's, in reference – not reverence – to a former caretaker of the cemetery whose shack sits abandoned near the spot where gravel leaves the blacktop. Small trees sprout from what was once the man's yard, his house leaning like a funhouse.

Paranormal investigator Ryan Straub, founder of the Missouri-based ghost-hunting group Tir Firnath, visits the cemetery often and has experienced strange things there. However, nothing has disturbed him as much as what he and friend Jeremy Taylor saw on that gravel road one autumn night. "It was, of all days Halloween 2000," Straub said.

He and Taylor walked around the cemetery for hours, waiting and watching under the gaze of the new moon. Nothing ghostly happened in the cemetery that night – but something did happen. "It was fairly cool out, the night was clear," Straub said. "Overall, the night at Hojo's was exceptionally boring. There was nothing out of the ordinary, and for there that was unusual." The two arrived at 10 p.m. and left at 2 a.m. That's when they saw the creature.

"As we were leaving, driving down the gravel road between two hills, on the road was a large, matted grayish-brown dog," Straub said. This was nothing unusual for mid-Missouri farm country. The large, dirty dog on the gravel road drew as much attention as a deer bounding from tree line to tree line. But this was no dog. "As we approached the dog it appeared to be hunched over something," Straub said. "Determined to go home after a boring night, we didn't want the dog to hinder our plans. We drove right up next to it."

Passing ten to fifteen feet from the animal, they flashed the truck's headlights at it. That's when the beast stirred. "The 'dog' stood up on its back legs and casually walked off the road," Straub said. In the cab of the truck, Straub and Taylor sat in shock as the beast walked across the path of the headlights on two legs.

"I wouldn't call it a dog exactly," Taylor said. "I mean, that's what we thought it was at first. However, it standing up on its two back legs and walking off the road casually ended the belief that it was a dog for me." As the beast stood, it turned to face the men staring blankly at it from the truck's cab. Both said it was taller than a man weighing about 250 pounds.

"The creature was roughly seven feet in height, grayish brown fur, muscular build," Straub said. "Its eyes were more of an orang-ey-yellow than just yellow. It smelt foul, like old moldy wet dog. The experience lasted maybe – maybe five to six minutes."

The thing that struck Taylor is that it didn't act like a beast; it acted more like a man. "The creature seemed calm, almost as if he understood the mutual inconvenience of eating in the middle of the road," he said. "It didn't seem or make any attempt to harm us. I was awestruck more then anything."

Straub and Taylor sat in the truck for nearly ten minutes, looking into the black, early-morning woods where the dog-like creature disappeared, walking like a human. "We sat there kicking ourselves in the ass for not getting it on film or trying to communicate or anything," Taylor said. "That was the most frustrating thing about it."

Neither Straub nor Taylor were afraid, it happened too quickly. "I felt more curious than anything. I didn't really have time to comprehend fear at that moment," Straub said. And he has only one explanation for it. "The only thing I could think of was it was the mythical beast the werewolf."

Werewolves, in various forms, have existed in many cultures across the world. From the Medieval European werewolf that dominates horror movies, to American Indian skinwalkers, the image of a man changing into a beast has terrified people for centuries. Most people think werewolves are legend. Some people – like Straub and Taylor – think that's dead wrong.

37

Bigfoot in Southeast Missouri

Darkness engulfed the Southeast Missouri farmhouse, the air still in the January night. Ken Mattheis knelt behind his parent's house working, meager light illuminating a generator, the only sign of electricity for miles. "A few years ago the power went at my parents' farm house and I went out to help them set up a generator for the first time," he said.

He'd left a tool in the van, so he walked into the darkness to retrieve it. "It was a cold, pitch black night," he said. "I heard footsteps on the ice-covered grass." He thought it was his father outside with him, but when a tree branch snapped, he knew it wasn't his father.

"I heard crunch, crunch, then limbs started breaking and falling," he said. "I turned to see what was causing the limbs to break and saw this large black shadow standing up under a tree behind me." The figure knocked down more limbs, then stopped. "It stood still as if it was waiting for me to do something," he said. "I thought, 'crap, you're not my dad.' So, calmly I walked away from it."

Mattheis backed inside the farmhouse. "My dad was inside the house," he said. "I told him, 'We have a visitor,' and he said, 'Who?' I said, 'A Bigfoot.'"

They looked out the window, but what Mattheis had seen was gone. It would be back. A few months later, Mattheis' mother saw something strange, and telephoned him.

"She said, 'Well the other night the dog was barking out by the fence and I went out to see what it was barking at and this large black shadow stood up and walked off into the woods,'" Mattheis said. "Now my mom says the dogs are afraid to go outside at night."

Mattheis went to the spot the next day and found large footprints in the grass. The heel of the foot had pressed deeper than the rest, the curve of the arch almost invisible. "I have photos of the tracks,"

The print from a Bigfoot that frightened Ken Mattheis' mother near Leasburg.
Photo courtesy of Ken Mattheis

he said. "Not great photos, but its big feet. Should have made casts of them but I didn't."

Bigfoot sightings aren't uncommon in Southeastern Missouri. According to reports, in the early 1980s, while camping near the Meramec River, a seven-year-old boy saw a large man-like figure covered in long, black hair near his campsite about seventeen miles from the Mattheis farmhouse. In late 2000, a group of campers saw a "massive" bipedal, hairy creature walking amongst the cabins of a campsite within twenty miles from the farm. Its arms were long and swung wide as it walked, its head crested like a gorilla's.

The specter of Bigfoot has been with Mattheis all his life. "My parents owned a home by my grandparent's farm in Crawford County and I spent summers in this home and spent a lot of time with them," he said. "My grandmother was Native American and she would yell at me and my cousins to stay out of the creeks or the Boogeyman will get ya." The young Mattheis thought she was just trying to keep the children away from the creek, so the warning made them want to go even more.

They soon found the warning had nothing to do with the creek. "A few times we went, we would hear something follow us and it would break tree limbs and this would scare the crap out of us kids," he said. "We'd run home and get swatted with whatever Grandma had in her hands at the time, and she'd say, 'Keep out of the creeks.'"

Another time, the thing sent Mattheis running until he was lost and a neighbor drove him home. He didn't see what had scared him at the creek until he was about ten years old. "I was sleeping in a bed with my older brother and we had the windows open," he said. "I heard sticks breaking and I lifted the shade to look out and I saw a large, light tan, shaggy-haired animal walk by the window and I said, 'What is that?'" His brother jumped up, shut the shade and told him to go back to sleep, it was only a deer. "I don't think he saw it," Mattheis said. "It scared the crap out of me."

A few years later, during a trip from town, he saw it in daylight. Mattheis and his cousin, Jim, had ridden their bicycles into nearby Leasburg, and Mattheis had a flat tire, so he called Grandpa. "My grandpa was in his 90s and he drove really slow," Mattheis said.

As his grandfather puttered down Route H, Mattheis and his cousin, sitting in the bed of the pickup, saw a man walking in a field. "I saw what looked like a large man in a light brown winter coat in coveralls with a hood up walking in a field," he said. "It was all light brown, the hair, face and hands was like the color of hay." The man was large and swung his arms like a cross-country skier. "We got closer and I realized it was a Bigfoot," Mattheis said. "The hair on top of the head was long and it went straight up and looked really strange like a Conehead."

The boys sat in the truck, staring at the Bigfoot as their grandfather motored by. The thing never looked at the truck. It just kept walking until it reached the woods. The boys didn't say anything to their grandfather, who didn't see the brown man walking in the field. Mattheis had a more personal experience a few years later.

"I had a truck and was with several of my cousins and his friends and we had nothing to do so I decided to go drive them into the woods that night and go listen for the panther screams," he said. "We drove into the woods and parked, and I think four or five kids were in back of this truck." After a few minutes of silence, the teens heard something large walking toward them through the woods. "We could hear something large in the woods coming towards us breaking limbs and breathing really loud in and out as if it had breathing problems," he said. "The kids freaked and wanted to leave, but I said, 'No, lets see what's coming.' I'd like to know what the hell is making all that noise."

The breathing thing circled the truck, breaking tree limbs and throwing branches toward the boys. "A kid laying down in back of this truck started punching my back window screaming at me if I didn't get us out of here right now he was going to drag my ass out of the truck and leave me here with it," Mattheis said. "I started the truck and turned on the lights and left in a hurry as I was more scared of this kid kicking my ass than whatever was in the woods."

Mattheis is convinced the thing circling the truck was a Bigfoot. He later bought a camera to take a picture of the beast that's life kept intersecting his own, but has yet to photograph one.

In the 1990s, Mattheis began using the Internet to communicate with Bigfoot researchers and met a researcher named Coonbo. "Coonbo was the first person that I know (who) claimed to be able to call them to show up," Mattheis said. "He would hoot like an owl and then we'd hear owl hoots back and we'd hear it coming through the woods and we'd smell the nastiest smelling musk and then we'd leave."

A heavy musk scent has long been associated with Bigfoot. "So I started doing this in Missouri and it didn't take long for me to call them to show up," he said. "My wife has a degree in anthropology and she thought I was just nuts for even thinking Bigfoot existed, so I took her into the woods."

They walked to the creek – the same creek Mattheis' grandmother warned him away from – and did an owl call. A call came back. "I said, it's going to circle us and come down this hill behind us and do another call,'" he said. "A few minutes later we heard a really loud 'who.' She said, 'That's not an owl,' and started crying and got into the car and said, 'Can we go home now?'"

Mattheis waited, telling his wife the thing that made the sound would go to the top of the hill and knock with a tree branch. It did. "She said, 'Okay, I believe they exist. Now take me home,'" Mattheis said. "She started crying and to this day she will not go into the woods at night."

38

The Great Time Machine Experiment

I have a time machine. That'd be a pretty silly thing to say if I didn't actually have one. I do. The story starts in the same place Sir Isaac Newton pondered the mysteries of the universe and Ernest Hemmingway went for inspiration. In a bar.

Blue, red, and yellow neon glowed softly on the tin-covered walls of this Northwest Missouri tavern as the waitress brought me a beer. The guys at the booth with me were having iced tea and Woodchuck Draft Cider. One was a chemist, the other a physicist. One of the great things about living in a small college town is having a beer with guys who have PhDs in chemistry and physics is no big deal.

And they had a proposition. More on that in a moment.

I don't know when I became fascinated with the concept of time travel. Maybe it was when I first saw Captain James T. Kirk order the *USS Enterprise* to slingshot itself around the Sun, maybe it was director George Pal's classic 1960 adaptation of H.G. Wells' *The Time Machine* (watch out for Morlocks), or maybe it was that growing up in the 1970s I wanted desperately to be anywhere else. All I know is before Marty McFly went back to the future, I was already hooked.

A few years ago, I heard a guy from Kansas on a talk radio program. He claimed to build and sell time machines. I wanted one. I just wasn't going to shell out $300 while the sane part of my brain laughed milk out its nose. I tried to schedule the time machine guy for an interview, but he wouldn't talk with me until I bought one of his devices.

Figures, right?

Steven L. Gibbs' Hyper-Dimensional Resonator in its original packaging.

"Let's apply for a grant," the PhDs said that day in the bar. "That way we can take the machine apart, study it, and write an article about it, and you can have your interview." A grant? Would a university actually spend money on something as frivolous as a time machine? Why yes, yes they would; especially since there are academic applications for it.

The proof is sitting in my office. But lets go back in time a bit – not with the machine, the normal way.

In 1981, Steven L. Gibbs, a farmer from Clearwater, Nebraska, received an interesting message – from himself. But this Steven L. Gibbs, he claims, was from another dimension and he had a diagram for a time machine called the Sonic Resonator. After building and testing the device, Gibbs, who now lives in Lyndon, Kansas, renamed the improved device the Hyper Dimensional Resonator and began selling them.

Patricia Griffin Ress, author of the book *Dangerous Information: The Further Time-Travel Experiments/Studies of Steven L. Gibbs*, met Gibbs in 1989. "I happened to meet someone who says, 'You should contact this guy,'" she said. She did, and invited Gibbs to bring his device to her home in Omaha. What she experienced made her a believer. "I interviewed Steve and he demonstrated the HDR," she said. Strange clouds formed in the room when Gibbs turned on the HDR and sparks danced around the chandelier.

No one time traveled, but something life altering happened to her that night. She later caught her favorite movie, *Shane*, on TV, but it wasn't the same movie she'd seen dozens of times. Dialogue she'd memorized was altered or spoken by different characters. It was the same movie, but it wasn't. "I have heard of movies filmed with two different endings, but I've never heard that before," she said. "It scared me to death. If you ask me to see the movie *Shane*, I'd say no thanks." She believes that night Gibb's HDR unit somehow altered the past ... and the present.

Testimonials from HDR users include trips from the 1850s, to sometime around 2012. Some "travelers" have claimed to return with objects from the past, but the objects have a short shelf life. "If you have something from a different time frame, it disintegrates," Ress said.

Gibbs' device also presents potential time travelers with other problems. "You have to have good intentions. If you were going to rob a bank and use it to get out of a bank, it wouldn't work," Ress said. "It would never work for that."

That's because Gibbs claims his HDR units work only with faith in God. "These coils," Gibbs writes in his catalog, "are specifically designed to pick-up and amplify soul-induced white light energy."

In 1997, Gibbs appeared on Art Bell's paranormal radio program *Coast to Coast AM* and spelled it out to an international audience. "Since the device, the way I believe, is tuned into the creator ... only the people who have pure intentions can use the device," Gibbs told Bell. "It takes your soul energy ... and steps it up through the diode circuit."

People using the HDR have reported going a few years into the future/past, being transported to Venezuela, dropped on-board a UFO, and have been thrown into a parallel dimension, Ress said. But the most troubling time traveler report, Ress said, is about a problem at the year 2012, the end date for the Mayan calendar. "They say right around 2012 it's like a brick wall," Ress said.

Although Ress hasn't witnessed anyone time traveling, she is convinced Steven's story is real. "You have a guy who in every way is an average farmer, now all of a sudden there's this average farmer studying quantum physics," she said. "This has all been very fascinating. I've reported on it and Steve asked me to write a book so he'd have something to sell when he's on TV."

The machine is a little black box with dials and three small switches. You're supposed to dial in the day, month, and year you want to travel to, although there are only two dials and they only go to ten. The directions frightened me. To use the time machine, place a quartz crystal in a well on the device along with a bit of spittle wrap (but don't use blood because that may conjure demons), wrap a coil cord around your head, place a strong electromagnet between your legs and rub a finger on a flat plate on the front of the machine.

As I sat in my office chair, rubbing my finger in circles on this little black box, electricity whirling around my head as the electromagnet hummed between my legs, I realized two things: 1) vasectomies make you brave, and 2) this isn't how Captain Kirk did it.

I didn't travel in time, but I was a bit light headed. A number of my students tried the machine, also. One even pricked her finger and placed blood in the well. No time travel, no demons.

The physics guys get to play with it next. I hope they don't run into any Morlocks.

Me feeling silly.

39

The Ghosts of Hillhaven

*V*ines crawl across flaking concrete walks that lead to a three-story building in Marceline, Missouri; long unkempt trees brush its red brick walls. The building, constructed in 1923, has served as the Putman Memorial Hospital, St. Francis Hospital, Hillhaven Nursing Home, and Meadowbrook Nursing Home, the final resident. It now serves as a playground for vandals and thrill-seeking teenagers. It may also still be home to all those who died within its walls.

Ryan Straub, founder of the mid-Missouri paranormal research group Tir Firnath, is more than familiar with the building. He spent a lot of time there as a boy; his mother, Patty Cruzan, worked there for ten years. "My mom says death comes in threes," he said. "The reason she says that is because of this place." At least ten people died in the building during her tenure. I hoped they were photogenic.

I met Straub in Marceline on a Friday in October. He came armed with a permission slip that allowed us to explore the building. "It was hard to get in for a while," Straub said. "The owner never wanted people in here."

Echoes greeted us as Straub pulled open the side door. The place is a wreck. Dust and plaster coated the parts of the floor we could see; furniture and refuse covered the rest. Now used as a storehouse, boxes filled with books are stacked or scattered throughout the first floor, holding titles like "Flowers in the Attic," "National Velvet," "Hunt for Red October," and dozens of Reader's Digest Condensed Books. Crossword puzzle pages dot the ground along with puzzle pieces nursing home residents once used to build landscapes. In one room, former St. Louis Cardinal Mark McGwire's smiling face stares blindly from the October 5, 1998 issue of *Sports Illustrated* that declares "70 Home Runs: What a Season."

Foliage is starting to claim the front of the Marceline nursing home Hillhaven that closed in 1998. Ghosts are said to walk the halls of this building.

One of the last magazines to arrive at Hillhaven, the October 5, 1998 edition of *Sports Illustrated*.

When Meadowbrook closed house, it left everything – desks, chairs, pots and pans, filing cabinets and beds. Vandals left the rest. "Cripps Rule" runs in spray paint across the walls of a stairwell between the first and second floor, although I'm not sure how many Los Angeles gang members live in this small mid-Missouri town. Empty, crushed cans of Natural Light are scattered throughout the building, every sink on the first floor is broken. "(The vandalism) has been cumulative over the last few years," Straub said. "I feel bad it's falling apart."

Cruzan worked at Hillhaven from September 1988 until August 1992 when Meadowbrook bought the building. In 1995, when Meadowbrook closed, the company hired her to "maintain the grounds and handle inventory," she said. She worked there alone until 1998. One night she received a call about the empty building; a light was on.

"My mom used to run the building," Straub said. "My mom would work up there during the day. There was no electricity."

One night, the police called Straub's mother reporting lights were on in the building and it looked like people were walking along the hallways. She was ill, so she asked Ryan to go by the building. "She sent me and a friend to figure out what was going on," he said. "We walked through the whole building. The lights were on when we went up there. There was one light on in one room on the third floor." As they approached the room on the third floor, they could hear the creak of a rocking chair on a hard floor. "The doors were very big and very heavy," Straub said. "We opened the door and there was the spirit of an old woman rocking back and forth. The sight of the apparition startled the two, but not like what happened next. "The woman who was facing the window without moving her body turned her head 180 degrees to face us," Straub said. "The smile was literally across her face. Her smile literally went from ear to ear. It was unlike anything paranormal I've ever seen." His mother later confirmed a woman had lived in that room.

Since that encounter, Straub has tried to banish spirits from the building, but whatever's there isn't ready to leave.

Straub quickly left, but he kept going back. He has investigated the building between ten and fifteen times and always encounters something beyond the ordinary. "There have been times I've been down here and all the doors in the hall were open and when I got to this door," he said, placing his hand on a door at the end of the second-floor hall, "they'd all shut."

Cruzan was with her son one day when this happened. "We went through that building, the doors were open," she said. "We went back, they were closed." She also knows of things that have happened in the building

Doors of this second-floor hallway have been known to slam shut on their own.

she can't explain. While a nursing home, third-shift workers occasionally reported hearing people walking upstairs, but when they checked on the sound, all the residents were asleep in bed. One worker said tasks she'd turned away from would be complete when she turned back to them. And Cruzan experienced something herself while she was there alone. "At one time I thought I heard something down in the kitchen," she said. "Something was going on down there, like somebody was there. I did go down there and didn't find anything. I didn't stay long."

People have reported being unable to breathe in certain parts of the building and footsteps can be heard running down the second floor hallway.

When I stepped into a room, Room 229, my chest suddenly grew tight, my breath labored. A curtain that once separated hospital beds began swinging as I stood in the room. Straub checked the windows and doors – nothing in the vicinity was open. There was no breeze. Straub and I changed places; the curtains still moved.

"I felt something in there," I said.

Straub nodded.

"Me, too."

Down the stairwell – peeling blue paint on the steps revealing bright orange underneath – we stepped around a cardboard box that sat sideways on the bottom step, paperback books spread out from its open top. Straub and I paused and asked each other about the box. It hadn't been there when we'd walked up the steps.

Dripping water from an earlier rain echoed through the bottom floor as we prepared to leave. Being alone in the empty nursing home, mold and decay taking firm hold of the once grand structure, we didn't feel alone. Straub said when his mother worked there, she was familiar with the feeling. "She always felt like there was somebody here," he said.

But Straub knows the strangeness of the building isn't because of people. It might be the building itself. "At night, it literally sounds like the building was growling," he said. "It feels like the whole building was growling. It almost feels like the building wants to mess with you a little bit."

The last time Straub visited the old nursing home; he saw a large dog print in the dust. "When I came down here with Mom they were all over the front room, but when I came through the next time, I didn't see them," he said.

"Maybe a vandal brought a dog with him," I replied.

"Not a dog with a seven-inch footprint," he said. "Seven inches in diameter. You just never know what's going to happen when you get here."

When Ryan and I walked down this stairway, we saw this box of overturned books. The box wasn't there when we'd walked upstairs.

40

The Girl in the House

*T*he house in Wood Heights, Missouri, built in the early 1970s, was quiet when Carol Spencer's family moved in on June 30, 1997. The town of 742 was quiet, too. Nestled in the softly flowing hills of Ray County, Wood Heights overlooks historic Excelsior Springs, home of the Elms Resort Hotel, where Harry S. Truman slept the night he won the 1948 presidential election. But something soon shattered the quiet.

"It wasn't too long," Spencer said. "Within the first six months I'd say. It actually started with my daughter. She would have been thirteen."

Spencer's daughter, Melissa, and a friend, were in the basement playing on the family's computer when they noticed something was wrong. "Chelsi and I were alone at the house one afternoon after school," Melissa Spencer said. "We had my stereo on in my bedroom, the volume up really loud." The music was loud enough in her upstairs bedroom the girls could hear it well in the basement, but they soon discovered the music wasn't loud enough. "As we were walking up the stairs, there was an eerie feeling," Melissa Spencer said. "Next, we heard a baby crying and then an older lady laughing."

The girls looked at each other, horrified, then ran out of the house to Chelsi's home down the street. "It got really loud and it really unnerved her," Carol Spencer said. "I didn't think anything about it. It's kids."

But the baby's cry and the old woman's laugh were just the beginning of the Spencers' experiences. "It seemed to be predominately in the den in the basement," Carol Spencer said. "We have a really tiny, tiny, tiny office that on the breaker box was labeled 'Grandma's Room.' I thought someone had died in the house."

Carol, an administrative assistant in the nearby Excelsior Springs School District, asked neighboring families about the prior occupants of the house. There were two or three owners, but no one died there and, if those families had any ghostly experiences, they didn't talk about it.

But something is wrong with the basement.

"Anyone who sleeps downstairs, if we have visitors from out-of-town they would be downstairs on the couches, they usually think they hear me hollering at them, calling them by name," she said. "They'll come upstairs and say, 'What do you want?' That happens a lot. The lights will turn on and off. That happens all the time."

Although no one died in the house, someone died in the neighborhood who was connected to the house. "When I got to checking into it, this girl got killed that lived around the corner," Carol said. "She spent a lot of summers here because one of the people who lived here had an above-ground pool and she practically lived here. I think she's searching for her family."

The girl, 11-year-old Michelle Osborn, was accidentally shot and killed by a cousin in 1981. Michelle Lowery, a special education teacher at Excelsior Springs Middle School, was a friend and neighbor of Michelle Osborn. "Growing up, I knew Michelle three years before she was killed," Lowery said. "When I moved to Excelsior, they were next door. Michelle and her sister, Jennifer; we became close. Michelle's parents were my second parents. We called their parents Mom and Dad."

Michelle was a prankster, Lowery said. "We would walk around the house looking for things that were ghosts," Lowery said. "We would set things up. She was ornery." Michelle's personality is one of the reasons Lowery is sure her childhood friend is still in the neighborhood. A few years after the accident, something happened in her room. "I know this was Michelle," Lowery said. "I had a friend spend the night. We had gone in my room, talking, giggling, being silly teenage girls."

Then it happened.

"I heard 'Missy,'" she said. "I asked Rachel, 'What?' She said, 'That was you.'" But it wasn't. Then a girl's voice that wasn't Michelle's or Rachel's said it again, "Missy." "It was from behind the dresser from over in the corner," Lowery said. "It sounded like Michelle. It was one of those things like someone was playing a joke on us. That's why I blame Michelle. She was a jokester."

Carol Spencer, whose house is across the street from Michelle Osborn's former home, is convinced the spirit in her house is

Michelle because she and her daughter Melissa Spencer saw her. "I was upstairs bathing one of the grandkids," she said. "I could swear I saw a person walk by and the dog even reacted to it." The girl was about the size of an eleven-year-old. "She was very petite," she said. "If it was the girl who was killed, that was about the right size."

Melissa Spencer saw the girl, too. "Both of us thought we saw someone walk down the hall," she said. "No one else was around. (The dog) was standing in the bathroom door looking down the hallway, too. Something must have passed by the door."

But there's something about the spirit in the Spencer house that doesn't act like an eleven-year-old girl. "I'm all the time working downstairs and I always think I hear my mother calling me and she'll be sound asleep," Carol Spencer said. "Mother lives with us and she won't go downstairs and do laundry after dark. She said, 'I refuse to go down there.'"

Although Carol Spencer isn't afraid of whatever haunts her home, it once made her uncomfortable. "At one point we had a sofa in the living room that made out into a bed," she said. "My husband snores really bad; some nights he'll sleep in the front room." One night, as she slept in her bedroom alone, something wrenched her from sleep. "It was like something heavy was over me," she said. "It was like darkness. It absolutely horrified me. I didn't see anything but it woke me up out of a sound sleep. That's the only time I felt that way."

Carol Spencer's sister-in-law from Weatherford, Texas, who, like Carol's daughter is named Melissa Spencer, is certain the thing in Carol's house isn't Michelle Osborn. One night, when she and her husband Jim were staying the night at Carol's house, something attacked her. "At Carol's, I didn't know about this thing in the basement," she said. "But I'm telling you, it's not that eleven-year-old little girl."

Jim and Melissa were sleeping in the basement when the thing that once woke Carol in terror, woke her in terror as well. "I woke up and I couldn't breath," she said. "Something was sitting on top of me, literally." Melissa and Jim were sleeping feet-to-feet on an L-shaped couch and, as a black cloud sat on Melissa's chest. Soon she began to hear music and the thing left her. "It went away for a minute and I started hearing this creepy music," she said. "I got up and went up the stairs to the kitchen. I thought they had the radio on." But the radio wasn't on. She looked at the kitchen clock; it was 3 a.m. She went back down the stairs, lay on the couch with her husband and fell into a fitful sleep. Then it struck again.

"I dozed off and when I woke up, whatever this thing is, it looks like a black mist," she said. "There was a little bit of light down there and I could see this form and it was holding me down." She couldn't talk and couldn't move much of her body, but she could move her feet. She kicked her husband until he woke. "I said, 'can't you see this thing?'" Michelle said. "He said, 'It'll be fine.' But it wasn't."

Struggling under the black mist, Michelle said to the entity that pinned her to the couch, "I'm God's property so leave me alone." And the mist dissipated. "The next day I told Carol and she told me the story of the little girl who got shot," Michelle said. "I said, 'This is not the little girl. It's something evil.' When I later went down those steps to go outside, I felt scared on the stairway. It was there."

Michelle's fears hit home when Carol Spencer told her about the prom picture.

"My son and his wife and three small kids stayed with us for three weeks and they stayed down there," Carol Spencer said. "My daughter-in-law was mortified. She felt something absolutely touch her. She put her head under the covers because she thought someone was down there." When her son and his family left, Carol Spencer found something even more frightening in the basement. "I found a little wallet picture of my son and her in a prom picture and something had pulled her head out," she said. "Just her head. The kids were teeny tiny and they couldn't do that."

The picture dragged terror across Melissa. "She showed it to me," Melissa said. "And I swear every hair on my body stood up."

Lowery, however, doesn't think something's wrong with the Spencer house; she's convinced something's wrong with the neighborhood. "I think this whole area, it's something about the area," Lowery said. "We've always tried to convince my mom there's something about (our) house. We've always thought our house had a ghost. Mom and Dad were like, 'whatever.'"

Then there's the Osborn house. The Osborns moved soon after their daughter's death and a hairdresser moved in. "My mom sent me there one day to get a perm," Lowery said. "It was in the basement. I always felt really freaked out in that house." Sitting in the chair, chemicals in Lowery's hair, the hairdresser excused herself. "When she was doing my perm she went upstairs for a minute," Lowery said. "I felt something was down there just looking at me. I remember feeling so scared I thought if (she) doesn't come back I'm going to leave." The hairdresser came back and finished the perm – Lowery ran home.

"All these houses are basically in the same (place)," Lowery said. "I wonder if these things are just in the area."

41

The Little Girl
of Arcadia Academy

Arcadia Valley Academy's red brick buildings aren't original to the campus, but they've still been there a long time. The academy, in Ironton, Missouri, opened in 1846 as a Methodist high school and served as a Union military hospital during the Civil War. However, it is best known from its later incarnation as a Catholic girls school that ran from 1877 to 1971. It also served as a convent for nuns of the Ursaline Order until 1985. It has most recently been a bed and breakfast and antique mall. Most of the buildings, such as the Administration building, the Auditorium, and the Gymnasium, were built between 1907 and 1934, and something unknown lurks in these buildings of the old Academy.

Belinda Clark-Ache, founder/owner of the paranormal investigation group Haunted Missouri Paranormal Studies, heard stories of a haunting at the 200-room academy and conducted a thorough investigation there. "We were there every month, April through October," she said. "I used to just go up by myself and rent a room for the night. All the potential; all the earmarks for a haunting were there."

... Such as a disembodied girl's voice that said "Lucy," and the presence of orbs. Although orbs, small balls of light captured by digital photography, are sketchy evidence at best – they can often be explained as dust particles, insects or moisture in the air – some are more convincing. Clark-Ache's group captured many orbs on video that were a mystery to them. "We got some interesting moving orbs," she said. "I'm not an orb person, but we have hours of video from the third floor hallway. One winter evening we had moving orbs up and down the hallway. We could never explain them away to our satisfaction."

Although Clark-Ache's group found some cursory evidence the Academy is haunted, they weren't entirely convinced. "I did an experiment the first few months. I would take (groups of visitors) on a walking tour of the place," Clark-Ache said. "I asked if anyone got any certain feelings. It turned out after about sixty people; we were averaging seven out of ten people feeling something out on the third floor senior hallway in the dormitory. But I didn't get anything compelling."

However, paranormal investigator Kim Luney, of Southwest Ghost Finders from Springfield, Missouri, did. Southwest Ghost Finders visited the Academy on invitation from Clark-Ache. "They did not tell us any history," Luney said. "We like to go in cold, investigate and hear the history later. It validates the findings."

Luney stayed in the Priest's room during her visit, across the hall from a paranormal investigation group from Posey County Clark-Ache also invited. "We kind of wandered around," Luney said. "We went in the Bishop's Room and snapped a bunch of pictures. Posey County showed up and we headed out of the room. I turned around and snapped a picture of the corner where a mirror was. I thought, 'I'll check it later.'" She was shocked at what she found.

"Later, I downloaded it onto my computer and there was the image of a child in that picture," she said. "You can see her eyes, her hair. You can make it out plain as day. I said, 'Oh, my God.'" No one else was in the room when Luney took the picture that appears to be a little brunette girl peeking at her from over the foot of the bed. "We tried to recreate it with actual people and you can't recreate that," she said. "It's obviously a child. It's just an awesome picture." While Luney downloaded the photograph, members of her team watching over her shoulder, the Academy again let them know it was aware of their presence. "You could hear footsteps out in the hallway," she said. "We'd look out the door and there'd be nobody there. When we went back in, we'd here little giggles like, 'I made them get up.'"

But Luney wasn't finished with the Bishop's room. Her group went there later in the evening to try and capture Electronic Voice Phenomena (inaudible voices that can be captured on tape) – and they did. "When we went back in the room later that night,

When paranormal investigator Kim Luney, of Southwest Ghost Finders, took this photograph no one saw this little girl. That's because the little girl wasn't there. *Photo courtesy of Kim Luney*

(a group member) said, 'I think we caught a picture of you,'" Luney said. When they listened to the recording later, they found the voice of little girl saying, "They got a picture of us." Maybe the little girl liked the attention; at 3 a.m., Luney was awoken by odd occurrences in her room.

"We were laying in bed and the bathroom door was opening and shutting itself for no reason," Luney said. "(I was) laying there and felt faint, feathery touches against the bottom of my feet. Then you would hear 'shss, shss, shss.' Like somebody was whispering to you, but nobody was there." The next morning, the owners said people have reported experiencing children running around their bed during the night. Luney said children died from influenza and cholera outbreaks and are buried on the Academy grounds.

But the most personal encounter Luney experienced was in the basement of the main building. "My team was creeped out," Luney said. "And if we feel creeped out, we don't go in." So they left, but not without audio recorders running. "When we were leaving the basement there was an EVP that said, 'Don't go, Kim.'"

Luney is convinced the Academy is haunted. "It's a great place," she said. "We went back a second time. There's little strange things that have happened, but we have to have evidence. If we don't, we throw it out, but the little girl was indisputable."

42

The Gregarious
Wade Brownfield

Smoke curled in front of the camera lens as Ken Billups, Jr. snapped shots of the Blue Springs Chamber of Commerce's October 2009 Business Card Exchange at the Dillingham-Lewis House Museum. But Billups didn't see the smoke. Picture after picture showed Chamber of Commerce members chatting throughout the building – a building in which no one is allowed to smoke. The white, billowing plume was in just one frame.

Donna Drake, archives and research chairman with the Blue Springs Historical Society, said it was the resident ghost. "When I took (Billups' picture) to two of the elderly women (who volunteer) there, they said, 'See. I told you there was a ghost here,'" Drake said. "He took tons of pictures in that area of the room. There wasn't anything on them but that one. I'm a very firm believer in ghosts."

General store owner Morgan V. Dillingham built the house in 1906, and lived there until his death in 1925. The two-story building made of native limestone has had multiple owners. The only person known to have died in the house, Arthur Frank Cummins, lived there from October 7, 1949 until March 31, 1966. Although others died while living in the house, details on whether they died inside the house are sketchy.

Blue Springs has always been a popular spot for travelers. For centuries, American Indians utilized the springs for which the town would later be named. Travelers West often stopped at the springs on their way to the nearby Queen City of the Trails,

The Dillingham-Lewis House Museum in Blue Springs, where a bearded man lurks in the bathroom.

Independence, Missouri. But many people decided to stay – some even after death.

Drake's grandson met one of them in the Dillingham house. "My nine-year-old grandson came over one day," Drake said. "He loves this house." At one point the boy went to the bathroom upstairs. A few minutes later Drake heard her grandson scream and looked up to see him running down the steps. "His eyes were big and he said, 'I saw the ghost,'" Drake said. "He said, 'I looked in the mirror and there was a man in there.'" Drake's grandson saw a man with a beard standing behind him, staring at him.

"I've been in there many, many times and have never felt anything," Drake said. However she has seen some things she can't easily explain. "A bunch of us were carrying Christmas stuff from the basement and we turned off the lights. But when we came up a lamp was on that none of us had ever turned on."

Then there's the hat and doors. "I've had things I know I've left them laying in a certain position," she said. "Like a top hat upstairs. I've had the top hat laying on the top of the couch and when I come in it was in the middle of the house. We have some closet doors. If you go up there and if you shut them and come back up, they're open."

This smoke that curled in front of Ken Billups, Jr.'s camera as he took this picture of the Blue Springs Chamber of Commerce's October 2009 Business Card Exchange. No one was smoking. *Photo courtesy of Ken Billups, Jr.*

It's not just hats and doors something unseen has touched, Mary Potter, president of the Blue Springs Historical Society said people have been touched as well. "At the last board meeting, (a board member) said, 'Mary, I thought it was you tapping me on the shoulder, but I looked over and nobody was doing it,'" she said.

Although Karol Witthar, who works at the Dillingham house, has never experienced anything ghostly there, she always says, "Hello, ladies, I'm coming up," before ascending the stairs. It's better, she figures, to be safe. "Not that I've seen anything," she said. "It wasn't until that picture; I didn't think about it."

However, the ghost of the Dillingham-Lewis House Museum might be a bit too gregarious to stay in one place. Numerous ghost sightings have been reported in the neighborhood, all connected to houses associated with the Dillinghams and Brownfields. David Dillingham, Morgan V. Dillingham's son, built the house next door to the Dillingham-Lewis House Museum. David's daughter, Margaret, lived there with her husband Wade Brownfield. "Four ghosts have been seen in the Brownfield house next door," Drake said. "I keep telling them the four ghosts – when they started (restoring) that house – they came over here."

And a ghost has been seen at another nearby house, where friends of the Dillinghams once lived. A recent occupant saw something sitting in her house. "She screamed. There was somebody in a chair," Drake said. "She said on the chair were these big, grubby hands. She said, 'there was something in this house.'" The figure sitting in the chair wore khaki work pants and shirt. Then she described the hands to Drake. "That sounds like Wade Brownfield to me," she said. "He just drops in where he wants to. He kind of dropped in on everyone in Blue Springs when he was alive."

Although Drake hasn't seen the ghost of Wade Brownfield or anything strange at the Dillingham-Lewis House Museum, she would like to. "I hope there is a ghost there," Drake said. "I would just love to have some experience with one. When I go in I always say 'good morning' and when I leave I say 'I hope you have a good evening.' If there's a ghost there, there's a friendly ghost."

43

J. Huston Tavern's
Thing in the Basement

*T*he J. Huston Tavern has stood in Arrow Rock since 1834. The two-story red brick building has been an inn, tavern, mercantile, and is now a state historic site and restaurant. Huston, a Virginian, built the Tavern as a home for his family and as a source of income. The Tavern is also home to spirits – and something dark.

A brick sidewalk runs between Main Street and the front of the Tavern. Seventy-nine people live in this town of antique shops, museums, and bed and breakfasts off U.S. 41 in Saline County.

Arrow Rock is on a bluff that at one time looked over the Missouri River, welcoming people traveling West, and has been home to painter George Caleb Bingham, Dr. John Sappington – the man who found the cure for malaria – and three governors. Today, visitors come to Arrow Rock to step back in history, see a Broadway-style show at the Lyceum Theatre, or maybe run into something ghostly.

Chef Liz Huff, proprietor of the J. Huston Tavern, knows ghosts walk the floors of the Tavern – she's seen them. "A ton of them," she said. "When I got here in January (2009) to set the restaurant up, I came in to bring in furniture and prints and my family quilts, and as soon as I started changing things this stuff started happening."

The first week Huff was in the Tavern, she stood in the front parlor when she saw something in the door glass. "I saw a woman's reflection," Huff said. "She was standing inside the dining room. She was wearing a white, long flowy thing. I can see her reflection

Ghosts and shadow people walk the floors of the J. Huston Tavern in Arrow Rock.

sweep across all the windows in the room." But there was nobody in the dining room to cause the reflection. "That scared me because that was the first thing I saw," Huff said, although she soon became comfortable with the spirits of the Tavern.

She discovered who the woman in white might be – J. Huston's daughter, Sarah, committed suicide nearby. "She almost died giving birth," Huff said. "She drown herself in the river. The idea is she comes back looking for her baby. But I don't know if that's who I see or not."

Huff sees figures in the Tavern at least five or six times a day, but she's not alone. "It's not just me who sees this stuff," she said. "It's everybody." People hear someone shuffling their feet in the lobby when no one is there and someone whistles in the middle dining room and the garden. Huff usually hears the whistle from the dining room in the mid afternoon.

Cody Hedrick from nearby Marshall has worked at the Tavern since July 2009 and heard the whistle behind the building. "There was whistling in the garden like someone was working," he said. "At first I brushed it off, but it got louder. It freaked me out."

Huff wasn't at the Tavern long before she also saw things move. Two clothing racks sit in the office upstairs, one rack holding chef clothing, the other holding period clothing – and the hangers move. "The rack with the chef clothes never moves, but the rack with the dresses moves," Huff said. "Everything will be still and all of a sudden the hangers will start moving, just on that rack." Some hangers sit dead still while hangers next to them move back and forth and still others spin. "The same thing has happened with pots and pans in my kitchen," Huff said. "The pot rack, we're talking six-gallon stock pots – big, big, heavy pots and pans – all of them will be still and one will be stirring on the hook. It's awesome."

Hedrick has also seen things move. "During days we just prepare there was one time I was looking at the swinging door and it started swinging," he said. "It was like someone pushed through it."

But the most apparent activity in the Tavern is the people. "There's a couple who likes to sit in the parlor room," Huff said. A table sits in the corner of the parlor room visible from the hostess station. Huff first saw the people in June 2009. "I was at the register talking to the hostess and I could see in the dining room," she said. "I could see two people sitting at that table."

The couple had their elbows on the table, propping their chins up with their hands and gazing into each other's eyes. Menus sat on the table in front of them but something was wrong. "Their water glasses had not been filled and I thought to myself, 'How long have those people been there and why is no one waiting on them?'" Huff said, but as she looked at them, they just disappeared. "Then no one was there. I just started laughing. It scared my hostess."

Huff has seen people walk past the coffee machine like they're going out the back door before disappearing into the kitchen. Unexplained noises are common in the Tavern and some people report a strange lavender smell in the building, but the most prevalent encounters are what Huff calls the Shadowy People and the Bright People. "The Shadowy figures are gray. They're just forms," Huff said. "They go through things, like I saw a Shadowy dude."

One day, as Huff walked toward the kitchen, a large "Shadowy guy with a hat" flew from the men's bathroom to the back dining room and disappeared. "He flew parallel to the floor about there feet off the floor," Huff said. "I thought it was funny because he was flying and the hat was still on him."

The Bright People are completely different. "I call them Bright People because I don't know what else to call them," Huff said. "You see a light and you see them for a second and they fade out again. I've never seen anything like this. They become a person for a second and then out."

Although Huff said these paranormal occurrences don't make her uncomfortable being in the Tavern at any time of day, that's not true for everyone. "We have something called the 'basement buddy system' because the girls don't like going down there themselves," Huff said. "It's not pleasant down there. It's scary. There's a heavy feeling down there like it's harder to breath."

People, including Huff, have seen a green light shoot through the basement. "There's a green light sometimes that flies across the room down there," she said. The first day she saw the light she was getting something out of the freezer, then she heard a bell ring behind her, but nothing was there. "I never tell people, especially the kids who work here," she said. "I never say something until somebody says something."

And they do.

Workers have also reported seeing the green light and hearing someone moving boxes in the basement when they're alone.

The basement is also the only place in the Tavern that bothers Huff – until something came upstairs.

"I thought the scary part was just down there and that's why I don't mind being here at night myself," she said. "But this summer I was here alone and I was closing up." As she walked through the kitchen, turning lights off as she made her way to the back door, she realized she wasn't alone. "I felt someone behind me, literally a half-inch away from my body," Huff said. "I was so scared to look back; I knew something was there but didn't want to see it. I just kept walking faster. I made it outside and was trembling."

Then she realized she didn't lock the cooler and had to go back inside. As she walked through the dark building, flipping lights on to see if anything was there, she grabbed the keys, locked the cooler and ran out. "You know those horror movies where people can't get the door locked because they're shaking?" she said. "It was just like that." Huff stood outside the back door, shaking, she locked the door and jiggled it to make sure it was locked and the door came open.

"Right when it opened I heard a 'clang, boom, boom' like some-one took the tongs and pans and were banging them together," she said. "I was so scared I went to my father's house. I didn't even go home. I didn't want to be there alone." It took a while before her father could get the story – Huff was shaking too hard to talk.

"I think whatever's in the basement came upstairs a min-ute," she said. "I want him to stay in the basement or go away. I didn't like it."

There might be a friendlier spirit in the Tavern, however. While Huff was on vacation in November 2009, Hedrick saw a man he didn't recognize. "Cody had a box of stuff and was walk-ing upstairs and he walked to the top of the stairs and looked up and saw a man standing in the ballroom," Huff said. "It was a solid human being." The figure wore a black jacket, ruffled shirt, knickers and a hat. Hedrick looked away, then turned back. The figure was gone. "That's a 1750s-1830s thing. That's not a pioneer thing," Huff said. "I've never heard anybody say they ever saw anything like that."

But Huff had seen that outfit before. Clay Marsh, a former proprietor of the Tavern, wore it on holidays and other special occasions. Marsh died of cancer in the mid-2000s. "It was ex-actly like Cody described," Huff said. It was the coolest thing. I thought wouldn't that be neat if it was him."

151

Afterword

What I hope you've learned from reading *Paranormal Missouri: Show Me Your Monsters* is that we, as the human race, really don't know much, do we?

For all our technology and scientific know-how, we still don't know if an eight-feet-tall, 500-pound species of primate is wandering around the forests of North America (or every continent on the planet, for that matter), if ghosts exist, if our planet is being visited by intelligent beings from outside our solar system. And why don't we know? Because the people who make the rules aren't looking hard enough. It wasn't until 1938 when a South African trawler captain showed a local museum curator a strange fish he'd caught that science rediscovered the coelacanth, a fish science thought became extinct 65 million years ago. Of course, the people of South Africa already knew that and found the coelacanth to be quite tasty. Maybe one day an anthropologist will stumble across a dead Bigfoot in the woods, or a full-bodied apparition decides to show itself to a physicist under laboratory conditions – over and over and over – or a UFO lands on the fifty-yard line during Monday Night Football (the White House lawn is out; nobody'd really notice). Then books like mine won't be about the unknown anymore; they will be about the known. Or maybe I'll just write about beer.

What should we do in the meantime? If you have a paranormal experience write about it, or contact someone who does. If you're simply interested in the paranormal, read about other people who've gotten the willies scared out of them. It's fun.

Or, you could try to experience the paranormal yourself. My first advice is don't. Depending on what aspect of the paranormal you want to investigate, it could be dangerous. Now, since we all know you're not going to listen to my first piece of advice, listen to the following advice – I make sense:

- Always ask permission to be anywhere. Seriously, anywhere. Even public places; you can be arrested for trespassing in a cemetery or park after dusk.

- Real live people are more likely to be dangerous than ghosts.

- Although ghosts don't usually seem to be dangerous, who knows? Depending on whom you talk to, ghosts are either the spirits of dead people, or are demonic beings. So, even if you see an entity that looks like Grandma, it could be something much more foul. Don't give it a reason to be attracted to you.

- Even though it's more fun to go somewhere purported to be haunted at night, go while it's light. It's a lot safer to have already scouted where missing floorboards or toppled, grass-covered tombstones may be when you run screaming through the dark.

- Take a flashlight, cell phone, knife, first-aid kit, food and water wherever you go. It's always good to be prepared.

- If you're going to be anyone from Scooby Doo, be Velma.

- Be observant.

- Try to explain everything naturally before settling on an unnatural reason.

- Study your subject. If you're scanning the skies for UFOs, knowing what conventional aircraft look like as they fly through the night might help picking the ordinary from the extraordinary.

- If you find a wallet with an undisclosed amount of cash without an ID, it's mine. Give it back.

So, did you go looking for the paranormal? Chances are you didn't find anything. But if you did, you're lucky. The paranormal only shows up in your life when it damned well feels like it. If you're looking for anything weird and find it, or if you just happen upon something strange, let me know about it at jasonoffutt@hotmail. com. I look forward to hearing from you.

A

My Experiences – All in Missouri

O ne of the first things I tell my reporting students at the university where I teach is nobody cares about the writer – they care about the story. That's almost always true, but writers are people and we become interested in certain topics for a reason. I became interested in the paranormal because the paranormal became interested in me. If it can happen to me, it can happen to you.

The following is a chronicle of the weird things that have happened to me in my life. I can't definitively say they were paranormal encounters, but I can say I can't explain any of them rationally. Although I usually shy away from a person who makes too many claims about their paranormal encounters (being abducted by aliens, seeing Bigfoot, and having an "inter-dimensional vortex" in their home is a bit much), mine are small and, in my case, I lived them. All of the following happened right here in Missouri, and these encounters are why this book is in your hands right now.

Age Eight

Daylight poured into my home on a Saturday afternoon, the blinds in this converted 120-year-old country schoolhouse pulled wide. I stepped out of my bedroom and into the hallway to grab a volume from our wall of *World Book* encyclopedias when I saw something that shouldn't be. There was a boy standing in the hallway. My family lived six miles from the nearest town and there wasn't a boy other than me within those six miles. The boy wore a blue flannel shirt and jeans, his brown hair mussed. The boy and I faced each other for what seemed like an hour, but it was more like seconds, when I realized what was going on – I could see the *World Books* on the bookshelf through him. The boy looked right at me, and he blinked.

I turned slowly, walked into my bedroom, shut the door and didn't talk about the encounter for thirty years. When I did, my family looked at me with dumb stares. They'd experienced nothing in that house (at least nothing they'd admit). I never researched the history of the house; I didn't, and still don't, want to know exactly who or what I saw. That would make it a little too personal.

Age Fourteen

My dad pulled into our farmhouse driveway well after dusk. After about twenty minutes, somebody thought to check why he hadn't come inside. We found Dad standing in the gravel drive by his rusty-brown Ford F-150 looking to the sky at a point over the field that separated our house from the farmhouse about a mile away.

"What are you doing?" Mom asked him.

He pointed toward a spot in the sky. "Do you see that?"

I did; so did Mom. Hovering over the field was a black spot that blotted out the stars on this clear night. And it was humming. After a few minutes staring at the thing, the telephone rang so I went inside and answered it. Our neighbor from across the field was on the line and he was standing outside his house looking at exactly the same thing. A little while later, the object moved away until it was gone from sight.

Age Twenty-six

When an assignment to cover a psychic convention in Kansas City came up, as a journalist interested in the world of weird, I accepted. People from all over the country were attending the convention, and at least one of them wore a pyramid on her head. But, as someone who's read a bit on the old-time Spiritualist movement, I wanted to interview Spiritualists who had a presence at the convention, so I walked away from the pyramid lady and found one. The Spiritualist pastor and I went into an empty ballroom for privacy and I was less amazed as I was dumbfounded at what she told me.

"How does someone become a Spiritualist?" I asked.

"In two ways," she said. "For example, they can be born into a Spiritualist family, much like you were born into a Methodist family and you are a Methodist."

She was right. I was Methodist.

"Or you can convert to Spiritualism," she continued. "Like your mother. She was Catholic and when she married your father, she became a Methodist."

If I stuttered while I thought, I would have done so at that moment. My mother was Catholic, and converted to marry my father. I'm not saying this woman was psychic or was receiving that information by communicating with the dead, but she couldn't have known what she said by conventional means.

Age Twenty-eight

I sat with three other guys in the unfinished basement of Victor's house playing cards. The doors upstairs were locked and we were the only ones in the house. After about the third hand, a woman's voice clearly said, "Victor," from a blank corner of the basement. We looked at each other dumbly – we'd all heard it.

There was no house where Victor's stood before his family built it ten years before, and no one knew if anyone had ever died there. Something, however, was there now. Except for me and the other two card players who finished the hand and left Victor home alone with something invisible that knew his name.

Age Thirty-six

Dark fields zipped past the car window as I drove home from the night shift at the newspaper. The approaching highway sign read "Orrick: 5 miles." As the green and white sign grew closer to the car, the song on the radio segued from something I wasn't paying attention to into "Gimme Shelter," my favorite Rolling Stones song. Cool. The drive was almost five minutes; the song was 4:30 minutes. I'd have company the rest of the way home.

The next thing I knew the car started dragging as the cruise control tried to compensate for a hill. But there were no hills between the road sign and Orrick. I turned off the car's cruise control I'd set at fifty-five mph and hit the accelerator. The car topped that hill, then another. I still didn't know where I was. A light shown atop a third hill. I pulled toward it and into the parking lot of a Jehovah's Witness church I recognized – it was five miles on the opposite side of Orrick. As I sat in the car, I realized "Gimme Shelter" was still on the radio. I'd driven ten miles and the 4:30-minute song was *still playing*. It played for another minute and a half.

Other than the road hypnosis, I have no idea what happened.

Age Forty

My telephone interview with Joyce Morgan, of Kingston, Missouri, was all over but the chatting. I'd never met Joyce, but I'd heard of her – she'd worked with police departments on murder cases and missing persons for twenty years and appeared on a number of cable TV shows. Before saying our goodbyes, she asked about the paranormal incidents that happened in my house. Funny, I hadn't mentioned it. The incidents involved my wife.

When my wife got up to go to the bathroom in the middle of the night, she would occasionally see a light that looked like Tinker Bell hovering over our baby's crib. One night, I saw it, too. So I told Joyce about it.

"Oh, that's just your grandfather checking on his namesake," she said, matter-of-factly.

I hadn't mentioned the baby's gender (a boy), I hadn't mentioned my grandfather's name, the fact that he passed away when I was small, or that we'd given our child the same name. But she knew. Somehow she knew.

Age Forty-two

The third floor of Laura J. Yeater Hall at the University of Central Missouri is closed due to electrical problems. It's also locked by a padlock. Although no one has had access to that floor but the housing department since fall 2001, the light in room 337 sometimes pops on for no apparent reason. Someone from the housing department has to go upstairs, unlock the door and turn the light off.

The day I visited the third floor of Yeater Hall, the director of the housing department took me there and, as we walked past room 337, we saw the light was on. The housing director, a bit surprised by the fact the light was on, put his finger on the switch and clicked the light off. We walked two doors down, turned around and came back. The switch was flicked up and the light was on.

The paranormal world is all around us. Strange things happen all the time, just keep your eyes open.

B

A Journey Through Time

Reporter David Tanner of Parkville, Missouri, wrote the following account of my 2004 past-life regression session with hypnotist Melissa McKim.

*J*ason Offutt always wanted to know if he had a past life. The author got his chance to go under hypnosis and regress into a past life in the name of healing. Although Melissa McKim of Soul Essence Healing in Kansas City did not uncover any serial killers or worse – politicians – in Offutt's past lives, she did evoke some powerful emotions.

"The habit pattern of the soul can repeat itself," McKim said. Her goal is to tap into that pattern and help her subjects heal from fears, pains, and traumas.

Here's how Offutt's session broke down:

Offutt met McKim at her office south of the Plaza for a one-hour session in past-life regression. On a comfortable couch, with pillows under his neck and knees for support, it didn't take Offutt long to reach a relaxed state. Relaxation means an open mind and a chance to let go of barriers. Offutt wasn't quite asleep, but he wasn't quite awake either. He would say later he remembered most of the question-and-answer session that followed.

"Pay attention to breathing," McKim said. "Inhale relaxation and exhale tension."

She walked Offutt through a series of associations, asking him to enter a room in his mind and describe the color of the lights he saw. At first, Offutt described a panicky feeling from being in the room. The white and blue energies made him anxious, he told the therapist.

"I feel like I did something wrong," he whispered.

In an effort to find the cause, McKim told him to imagine a porthole that he could look through as an observer.

"Trips back in time are guided by the higher self, which knows everything about you," she said.

As the session elapsed, Offutt began to see himself at a fair, waiting to meet a girl and propose to her. He then described a marriage and a simple farm life. As McKim questioned him about his feelings, Offutt described a child that died at birth. It was shocking to the family.

"She cries," he said.

Offutt said as the years passed, his wife's depression led to suicide at age forty. McKim asked him to fast-forward to his own death, where Offutt described dying drunk and alone. Tears streamed down Offutt's cheeks. He said he remembered a tear dripping into his ear as he lay on the couch.

Trying to change pace from the traumatic visions, McKim turned the session around, coaxing her subject to release the pain.

"Release ... recharge," she said.

She took him on another journey. This time, Offutt described a man having a successful business in a small town. But again, Offutt's emotions began to dwell on the negative. McKim asked Offutt why the dream turned negative. "He doesn't feel he deserves the happiness," came the response.

Offutt said he didn't know why he felt that way.

McKim then led Offutt out of his dream state, coming back through rooms with different lights and words of release and recharge. Returning him back to the land of the living, McKim asked Offutt to wake up and sit up under his own steam. After a drink of water they discussed the session, which lasted about ninety minutes.

"A few times I felt like I was put in a corner," Offutt said. "The fight-or-flee feelings take over."

Offutt said he experienced tightness in his chest at one point. McKim said everything that surfaced during the session can be interpreted differently. Mainly, she said, there was nothing abnormal about the session or the things Offutt saw in his hypnotized state.

"With a past life or the subconscious, we don't know if it's real or a fable teaching us something," she said. "Sometimes it's like opening a very small Pandora's Box."

McKim, who sees several clients per week, said most people can be hypnotized.

"Sometimes, it's the right time, and sometimes it's not," she said.

Offutt said he would do a past-life regression again, if given the opportunity, because it piqued his curiosity.

"It amazed me," he said. "Things I never thought of before came into my head."

———————————————

Soul Essence Healing can be reached at (816) 374-5988.